The Pocket Encyclopaedia of

BUSES AND

TROLLEYBUSES

BEFORE 1919

BY
DAVID KAYE

LONDON

BLANDFORD PRESS

First published 1972
© 1972 Blandford Press Ltd.,
167 High Holborn,
LONDON WC1V 6PH

ISBN 0 7137 0565 5 ✓

*Dedicated to Bill Cable-Scott, who through his
study of trams instilled in me a love for the old'uns*

Colour section printed by D. H. Greaves Ltd.,
Scarborough
Printed and bound by C. Tinling & Co. Ltd.,
London and Prescot

CONTENTS

ACKNOWLEDGEMENTS

Thanks are due to the following for having kindly supplied photographs for use in this book: Barton Transport, Birmingham Corporation, H. Brearley, J. Carman, D. Chalk, Chessington Zoo, Derby Corporation, Department of Education and Science, Dundee Art Galleries and Museums Dept., Edinburgh Corporation, W. E. R. Hallgarth, Hull Transport Museum, Imperial War Museum, D. W. K. Jones, Karrier Ltd., Lancaster Corporation, Leeds Corporation, London Transport Executive, R. C. Ludgate, Museum of British Transport, Museum of Transport (Glasgow), J. Nickels, M. P. M. Nimmo, D. Pennells, R. Perry, Scottish Omnibuses, the Shuttleworth Collection, R. H. G. Simpson, H. J. Snook, Stockport Corporation, Tramway Museum Society and West Bromwich Corporation. In addition coloured transparencies were provided by Museum of Transport (Glasgow), D. Kaye and M. Rickitt.

PREFACE

THIS three-volume series of pocket encyclopaedias covers the history of the British bus, coach and trolleybus from their inception until 1968. This book opens when the first Elizabeth was on the throne and people were just beginning to travel along the rough tracks that were the high-ways of those times, in vehicles which lacked springs or even any padd-ing to their wooden seats. The coach was just about to evolve out of the cumbersome medieval carrier's waggon. We trace the development first of the coach waggon, then of the stage coach, and finally of its speedy successor and deadly rival, the mail coach. We watch the three separate attempts that were made to supersede the horse drawn bus and coach with a steam driven one, and then we concentrate on the multitude of petrol-engined motorbuses and charabancs that suddenly appeared during the ten years that led up to the First World War. Nor do we ignore the advent of the trolleybus and the various hybrids that appeared briefly on the transport scene, such as the petrol-electrics and the electric-battery buses, though of these it has only been possible to include a selection.

While researching for this early period I came across conflicting reports about some vehicles, and I have put down in print what I consider on reflection to be probably the correct data; but I am open to argument, and would welcome any constructive comments that the reader may have in this field.

I wish publicly to acknowledge my debt to a number of senior mem-bers of the omnibus enthusiast fraternity, especially to Harold Brearley, Edmund Gaffney, John C. Gillham, George Hearse, Charles E. Lee and John F. Parke, without whose help I should have been unable to complete this book. I must also pay a tribute to all those general managers and other officials of the longest established municipal, inde-pendent and nationalised bus operators who kindly supplied me with information, often having to spend much time consulting their records in order to do so.

Grantham   David Kaye
Autumn 1971

A.E.C. = Associated Equipment Company
B.E.T. = British Electric Traction
b.h.p. = brake horse power
B.H. & P.U.O.C. = Brighton, Hove & Preston United Omnibus Company
B.S.A. = Birmingham Small Arms
B.T.H. = British Thomson-Houston
G.E.R. = Great Eastern Railway
G.W.R. = Great Western Railway
L.G.O.C. = London General Omnibus Company
L.M.O.C. = London Motor Omnibus Company
L.N.W.R. = London North Western Railway
L.R.C.C. = London Road Car Company
L.S.W.R. = London & South Western Railway
M.E.T. = Metropolitan Electric Tramways
m.p.g. = miles per gallon
N.E.R. = North Eastern Railway
P.A.Y.E. = pay-as-you-enter
p.s.i. = pounds per square inch
p.s.v. = public service vehicle
R.A.C. = Royal Automobile Club
R.E.T. = Railless Electric Traction
r.p.m. = revolutions per minute
S.M.T. = Scottish Motor Traction
U.D.C. = Urban District Council

INTRODUCTION

'It is hard to imagine any more dreadful sort of conveyance than a whirlicotes wagon [of the 15th century], yet it was the strict preserve of the greatest ladies in the land, who must be sheltered from the common gaze as well as from the wind and rain and the mud of the road. There was one virtue in it; though the bumping must have been terrific, and sticking axle-deep in the mud a frequent event, the "carriage" was so uncompromisingly broad and substantial that it was less likely than many of its successors to overturn.' (C. Hamilton Ellis, *Popular Carriage*, London, British Transport Commission, 1954, p. 4.)

Writing of his experiences on the Chester to London stage coach two centuries later in 1657, a Lancashire parson lamented, 'This travell hath soe indispoed mee, yt I am resolved never to ride agayne in ye Coatche.' However, apart from the Plague Year of 1665, the Chester stage continued to run until it was ousted by the railway. By 1770 the experts had improved the vehicle almost out of recognition, but the famous agricultural journalist Arthur Young could still cry out that the roads in the North of England were 'Infamously bad – most execrably vile – impossible to describe . . .'. However, even the roads were beginning to respond to treatment. After Telford had finished his work on renovating the London to Holyhead road, for instance, it was possible for the passengers bound for the Irish boats to travel the 261 miles in 26 hrs 55 min. at an average speed of 13 m.p.h. Mind you this did necessitate no less than 27 changes of horses!

Cut throat competition slashed the times taken on journeys, so that whereas in 1657 the parson mentioned above took four days over his ordeal from Chester, by 1754 the 'Flying Machine' from Liverpool to London took only three days to cover the 206 miles. Another instance of time paring is that on the east coast run to Edinburgh. In 1734 the 'Flying Coach' covered the distance in twelve days, but by 1773 this had been cut by half.

The arrival of Palmer's Royal Mail coaches in 1784 hotted up the pace considerably, his own vehicle cutting another hour off the already good time between Bath and London. Falmouth in far off Cornwall was brought within 35 hours of London on the Mail, and

Edinburgh enjoyed the 'Sixty Hour Coach' between the two capitals by the end of the 18th century.

Nevertheless, apart from the condition of the actual coaches and the state of the roads, there had been other hazards to deter all but the most hardy (or foolhardy). Stella Margetson in her book *Journey by Stages* recalls some of them (p. 69): 'From Stamford, the coach passed the turnpike gate at Horn Lane, from Lincolnshire into Rutlandshire and back again into Lincolnshire across Witham Common, a notorious stretch of the road for highway robbery, to the Black Bull at Witham Corner and down the steep and dangerous Spitalgate Hill into Grantham, one hundred and ten miles from London. Here there were several inns of outstanding quality and the Angel, going back to the 13th century, was said to be one of the first in the kingdom. Here also, between supper and going to bed, travellers not too exhausted by their journey could find entertainment at the theatre, which was patronised by the local gentry and visited by Garrick himself on his summer tours.'

By 1820 there were about 1,500 coach departures from London every 24 hours. Indeed if you had stood at Hyde Park Corner that year something in the region of 300 stage coaches would have passed you on their outward journey each day. No less than 84 coaches plied to Birmingham, 70 to Manchester, 40 to Brighton, 30 to Edinburgh, 19 to Chester, 18 to York, 13 to Glasgow, 12 to both Hull and Preston, and 9 going as far as Aberdeen. In the previous year the stage coach had reached the northern tip of the mainland when a service was started to Thurso.

In 1825 the Shrewsbury 'Wonder' increased the tempo of stage coach competition further by completing the journey of 158 miles to London in one day. But records now tumbled fast and furiously. 1832 saw the Birmingham 'Tantivy' covering the 125 miles to London in just twelve hours, whilst the very next year the Manchester 'Telegraph' took only seventeen hours to cover the 186 miles to the capital. There were accidents due to speeding, and in 1820 a race between the Chester Mail and the Holyhead Mail led to the death of a passenger (William Hart), resulting in the two coachmen (Thomas Perdy and George Butler) being sentenced to a year's imprisonment each at the Hertford Assizes. When it is realised that, for example, the Shrewsbury 'Greyhound' ran with one horse totally blind, it is surprising that there were not more fatalities. Such coaches as the Brighton 'Sovereign' and the Edinburgh 'Strathmore Union' had exceptionally low-slung bodies with small wheels and a wide track to ensure a safer ride. To reduce top heaviness a special compartment was built for the outside passengers. A clergyman from Hartford Bridge (near Crewe) invented another kind of coach, the small wheels of which were designed to discourage overturning on rough roads. A Birmingham man designed a tripping hook that released horses from their shaft as soon as the coach capsized, thus lessening the resultant carnage.

Some of the vehicles introduced during the closing decades of the coaching era were certainly strange. Between Glasgow and Greenock ran the 'Royal Oak', which was a double-decker that looked rather like an early tramcar: pulled by six horses it sat 40 passengers. Then there was the 'Royal Caledonian Basket', the extra long chassis of which enabled an equally extended body with seats for 26 to be fitted. Also in Scotland, John Croall of Edinburgh in 1806 had a waterlogged barge removed from the Forth-Clyde Canal, fitted wheels on to it, and ran it between Stirling and Slamannon, with the added attraction of a Negro coachman to drive it.

The terminus for coaches bound north from London was the Bull & Mouth (originally called the Boulogne Mouth). It was run in the fading days by Sherman. By 1842 only three of his former 73 daily departures were left. Similar fates had befallen his colleagues, who ran the other two main London coaching terminii: the Belle Sauvage (named after Princess Pocahontas) and the Bolt in Tun. The Royal Mail was removed to the railway for the run to York and Newcastle in 1842, and two years later the Dover Mail, the last out of London, also ceased to run because of railway competition. In 1847 the Newcastle to Edinburgh section was also converted to railway operation. The following year the 'Bedford Times' made its last journey. However, some few routes did survive the 'railway mania' of the 1840s. For instance, a three-horse stage from Amersham and Wendover ran daily to the Old Bell in Holborn until 1890, when the extended Metropolitan Railway line to Aylesbury forced this route too to succumb. Even then there were still a few stages left in Britain, the very last apparently being the 'Duchess of Gordon', operating from Fort William. This ran for the final journey on 29 May 1915.

The advent of the railways may have meant the end of the majority of stage coach and mail coach routes, but the horse drawn public service vehicle was still very much alive for other purposes than long distance express work. There were the short distance stages, like Billing's route between Elstree and London. If we take two towns at random we can see what the picture was like in 1836. Alan Bates has recently compiled a *Directory of Stage Coach Services* for that year (David & Charles, 1970), and readers are recommended to consult this masterful work of research for examples from their own area. In Wales, there were four short stages out of Abergavenny to surrounding places: E. Pinchase operated to Merthyr (20 miles), J. Barnett to Monmouth (12 miles), E. Lewis & Company to Newport ($22\frac{1}{2}$ miles) and T. Heath & Company to Ross (26 miles). These were daily routes with one journey in each direction. Apart from Barnett's 9-seater single-decker, the remainder ran 8- or 9-seat double-deckers (i.e. normal small stage coaches). Indeed some express stages ended their days doing these runs – for instance, the Cardiff to London stage (see Plate 3) after 1845 ran between Cardiff and Newport, Mon. Up in Lancashire the inhabitants of Aintree were not so fortunate as their Welsh cousins. S. Towers ran an 18-seater on Saturdays only to Crosby, whilst the remaining routes ran on Mondays only to Knotty Ash (M. Dickerson), Old Swan (J. Bunnell), Prescot (J. Holden) and Woolton (J. Newton). In all these cases the vehicle used sat 12 passengers.

The other main use of horses was for local routes, first as 'short stages' linking villages with the larger towns, then as omnibuses which plied for hire along the route. The earliest of the latter is credited to George Shillibeer, who began to run between Paddington and the Bank on 4 July 1829. He even provided his clientele with free newspapers to read while they jogged along between Paddington and the Bank, and at first the conductor on the bus was dressed as a midshipman and was fluent in both French and English to assist the tourist and entertain the élite. The fare of one shilling was modest compared with the exorbitant rates charged by the hackney carriage drivers – 3s. 2d. from Hyde Park Corner to the Bank, for instance, in 1806. By 1836 Shillibeer was operating three 12-seaters from Islington to the Elephant & Castle, four 15-seaters from Oxford Street to Greenwich, a further two 15-seaters on the Bank to Edgware Road (Paddington) route, one more from Oxford Street to Woolwich, and an eighth 15-seater between Greenwich and Woolwich. But by 1836 there was keen competition on many London routes, the Bank to Paddington route alone attracting nineteen other rivals owning 50 licences, and running no less than 272 return journeys daily.

The advent of the horse tram, first on Southend Pier in 1846, then in the streets of Birkenhead (1860) and London's Bayswater Road, Victoria Street and Kennington (1861, but only for short periods), made it look as if the horse-drawn bus was doomed after quite a brief life. However, as new tramways were laid down, so the horse bus adopted a new urban role as a feeder to tram terminii, in places where the population was not yet large enough to warrant the capital expenditure required to lay down permanent way. The horse tram came to the principal British towns as follows:—

1862　Darlington, Potteries (Hanley to Burslem)
1865　Portsmouth
1869　Liverpool
1870　London (a permanent basis)
1871　Edinburgh, Leeds
1872　Belfast, Cardiff, Cork, Dublin, Glasgow, Plymouth, West Bromwich
1873　Birmingham, Sheffield
1874　Aberdeen, Leicester, Middlesbrough, Newport (Mon.)
1875　Bristol, Kingston upon Hull
1876　Douglas, Wrexham
1877　Dundee, Manchester, Salford
1878　Newcastle upon Tyne, Nottingham, Wolverhampton
1879　Chester, Gloucester, Preston, Reading, Southampton, Sunderland, Wallasey
1880　Bolton, Derby, Ipswich, Tynemouth, Wigan
1881　Northampton, St. Helens
1882　Bradford, Chesterfield, Exeter, Gosport
1883　South Shields
1884　Worcester
1885　Paisley

The other threat to the horse bus came from the steam carriage. During the early 1830s in London and the early 1870s in Edinburgh attempts were made to design safe, capacious, speedy steam propelled vehicles, either with the engine incorporated as part of the carriage, or with a drag or tractor towing a passenger trailer. Owing to mechanical faults, scaremongers spreading rumours of imminent explosions (they did sometimes occur, but not as often as some would let people believe), prohibitive tolls and, finally, quite unnecessarily harsh regulations on speed, the heyday of the steamer in public road transport was delayed until the repeal of the so-called 'Red Flag Act' in 1896. Yet would-be steam bus proprietors had to watch one town after another adopting the steam tram without any trouble with the authorities at all. Although

Bristol's step in this direction in 1880 lasted less than one year, and the Ryde Pier steam trams lasted only from 1881 to 1884, when horses were brought back (they had done the work since 1864), the other early essays in steam tramway succeeded. Their dates were as follows:

1876   Wantage
1877   Swansea, Vale of Clyde (Govan)
1879   Guernsey
1880   Dewsbury, Leeds
1881   Blackburn, Burnley, Darwen, Edinburgh, Potteries (Longton to Stoke), Stockton on Tees
1882   Belfast, Birmingham, Bradford, Wigan
1883   Bury, Gateshead, Huddersfield, North Shields, Rochdale
1884   Coventry, Dudley, West Hartlepool
1885   Barrow, Dundee, North London, Oldham
1886   Accrington
1887   Haslingden, Rawtenstall, Wolverton
1888   Dublin
1889   Bacup, Kingston upon Hull
1890   St. Helens

Hardly had the steam tram got under way when another and more deadly rival to the bus appeared on the scene: the electric tram. On 4 August 1883 Magnus Volk started his line along the sea front at Brighton, and this was shortly followed by the Giant's Causeway electric tramway in Northern Ireland. This carried its first passengers in November of that year. Two years later another electrified Irish line opened between Bessbrook and Newry. September 1885 also witnessed the opening of one of the most famous electric tramway systems in the world: Blackpool's. On 7 September 1893 the Manx Electric Railway began its line between Derby Castle (Douglas) and Groundle Glen, a line that was to extend seventeen miles to Ramsey by 1899. The Snaefell Mountain Railway followed in August 1895. Gradually horse and steam trams were replaced by the new electric marvels. Thus in the case of the famous Mumbles line near Swansea, just as the reign of the horse had lasted from 1807 until 1877, so the reign of the steam tram was terminated in 1929, when the line was electrified, eventually to carry the largest-ever tramcars (106-seaters) to run in Britain.

Before we pass on to the beginnings of the motorbus, let us pause and read two contemporary reports on the horse omnibus scene. The first comes from the pen of the Victorian naturalist and traveller

Richard Jefferies, writing in his book *Open Air* in 1885. Under the chapter entitled 'A Wet Night In London' he states: 'The 'bus-driver, with London stout, and plenty of it, polishing his round cheeks like the brasswork of a locomotive, his neck well wound and buttressed with thick comforter and collar, heedeth not, but goes on his round, now fast, now slow, always stolid and rubicund, the rain running harmlessly from him as if he were oiled. The conductor, perched like the showman's monkey behind, hops and twists, and turns now on one foot and now on the other as if the plate were red-hot; now holds on with one hand, and now dexterously shifts his grasp, now shouts to the crowd and waves his hands towards the pavement, and again looks round the edge of the 'bus forwards and curses somebody vehemently. "Near side up! Look alive! Full inside" – curses, curses, curses; rain, rain, rain, and no one can tell which is most plentiful'.

The other extract comes from *The Bus, Tram & Cab Trades Gazette* for 29 October 1898: 'Everybody rides in omnibuses in these democratic days. The character of these useful public vehicles has entirely changed during the past few years, and the old lumbering fusty-smelling coach with its manifold drawbacks has given place to a clean, roomy conveyance in which the comfort of the passenger is studied in every way.'

The very first issue of *The Commercial Motor* on 16 March 1905 contained this significant sentence: 'Beckenham tramway scheme has been abandoned, with a view, it is stated, of adopting a motor omnibus system.' In that same inaugural number Col. R. E. B. Crompton wrote an article 'in favour of the motor omnibus' in which he listed the following advantages that he felt it had compared with its arch rival the electric tramcar, viz.:

  (i) greatly increased speed (i.e. 12 m.p.h. compared with 7 m.p.h.)
  (ii) lower cost (for purchase of equipment)
  (iii) less noise
  (iv) reduced interference with other traffic
  (v) capacity of motorbuses to work a less frequented route, and then to be temporarily transferred to heavily trafficked routes to relieve congestion.

The descriptive text that follows this introduction deals with many of the earliest battery, steam and petrol-engined omnibuses that were tried out between 1889 and 1902. Most is known about those that were employed in London, but it must not be forgotten that other less well known experiments also took place. For example Thomas Henry

Barton, a trained engineer from Nottingham University, began a service using a 6-seater Benz-Campion waggonette at Mablethorpe in 1898. In that year motor cars were licensed as p.s.v's for a service between Torquay and Paignton. A Lifu steam bus operated at Mansfield, whilst Falkirk and Llandudno were two other towns to witness the teething pains of the motorbus. The earlier editions of *The Commercial Motor* are full of proposed new motorbus operators and routes. An example is the Isle of Wight Express Motor Syndicate Ltd., who with seven Milnes-Daimler 36-seat double-deckers in 1905 proposed to run four routes on the Island, viz.:

route 1: Ryde–Bembridge–Shanklin–Godshill–Carisbrooke–Binstead–Ryde.
route 2: Ryde–Newport–Totland Bay
route 3: Cowes–Osborne–Binstead–Ryde–Brading–Sandown–Ventnor–Niton.
route 4: Cowes–Parkhurst–Carisbrooke.

However, there were several novel and enterprising features about the service offered by this company. Large baskets capable of carrying 5 cwt of parcels were fixed above the driver's cab; post boxes were attached to the exterior of the nearside of each bus next to the rear platform; five shilling rover tickets were instituted. No wonder that Lady Adela Cochrane, the wife of the island's Deputy Governor, inaugurated the service at Ryde Esplanade. However, neither did it deter the local magistrates four months later from fining a driver £2 with one guinea costs for driving at 18¾ m.p.h. along the main road between Ryde and Sandown.

Elsewhere firms mushroomed up during 1905: the Peterborough Motor Bus Company, the Southend-on-Sea & District Motor Omnibus Company, the Mid-Sussex Motor Company, the East Kent & Herne Bay Motor Omnibus Company, the Durham & District Motor Omnibus Company. In some places the influential local people gave such ventures their support (e.g. the Mayors of Dunstable and Durham), but on 5 July 1906 the editor of *The Commercial Motor*, under the sub-heading 'Delays are dangerous', sounded a note of warning: 'At least half-a-dozen projected motorbus companies appear to have fallen through during the last three months. Of these we may cite the proposals for a service between Dunstable and Luton, and one in the Bromley district.' It was further pointed out that such delays make the public suspicious – suspicions that were perhaps confirmed for some by the famous and tragic accident that occurred to an L.M.O.C. double-decker that got out of control and crashed with the loss of ten lives on Handcross Hill in July 1906. The fact that a B.H. & P.U.O.C. Milnes-Daimler rushed doctors, nurses and stretchers from Brighton to the scene of carnage within one and a half hours, did little to counterbalance this shocked mood. No wonder the Editor had cause to condemn the Blackpool Sea Front Omnibus Races, staged in October of that year. During these sprints for the standing mile and flying kilo-metre events Critchley-Norris, F.I.A.T., Leyland and Ryknield buses participated. This was the 'railway mania' all over again, and it was not surprising that in July 1908 Kent Motor Services had reluctantly to withdraw their 30-seaters from their Maidstone to Sutton Valence and Sittingbourne to Faversham routes, and to substitute smaller and more economical 12-seaters. Another Kent operator, J. W. Gunn of Swans-combe, solved the problem by buying sixteen second-hand Scott-Stirlings from the London Power Omnibus Company, and converting them so that when they were not conveying passengers between Gravesend and Swanscombe, they were carting strawberries to Covent Garden!

On 12 April 1903 world history was made at Eastbourne when the municipality began the first motorbus service to be *owned* as well as run by a corporation with some Milnes-Daimlers. (Southampton Corpora-tion had run *hired* buses from 5 August to 20 December 1901.) Bolton Corporation followed in 1904 with some Scott-Stirlings, and in September 1905 Wolverhampton followed suit with a Wolseley. 1906 saw Bournemouth (Straker-McConnell), Leeds (Belsize-Ryknields), Manchester (Leylands) and Nottingham (Thornycrofts) commencing motorbus routes. In 1907 it was the turn of Haslingden (Leylands), Rawtenstall (Moss & Woodd 'Orions') and Todmorden (Critchley-Norrises). Hull (second-hand Saurers), Keighley (Commer CCs) and Widnes (Commer CCs) joined the 'club' in 1909, with Liverpool trying out a mixed bag in 1911. Halifax started with the Daimler Y in 1912, whilst the next two years saw a tremendous advance in municipal motorbus operation, viz.

1913   Birmingham (Tilling-Stevens TTA1s)
          Middlesbrough (Bristols)
          Oldham (Tilling-Stevens TTA1s)
          Rotherham (Daimlers)
          Southport (Vulcans)

                    Warrington (Tilling-Stevens TTA1s)
1914   Chesterfield
                    Coventry (Maudslays)
                    Edinburgh (Leylands)
                    South Shields (Edisons)
                    Southend-on-Sea (Straker-Squires)
                    West Bridgford (Dennis)
                    West Bromwich (Albions)

At the outbreak of the First World War this process slowed to a trickle. In 1915 Walsall began with Tilling-Stevens TS3s, and the next year Lancaster started with three Edisons.

1903 also witnessed another significant advance on the motorbus front when the Great Western Railway Company began the first of their rural routes to feed their train services. On 17 August four small 16-h.p. Milnes-Daimlers began to run between Helston and The Lizard, followed on 31 October by a second route between Penzance and Marazion. Most of the early routes were in the West Country, but on 18 July 1904 two vehicles began operating the three miles between Windsor and Slough, followed on 5 April the next year with a route from Windsor to Ascot. On 1 July 1905 the G.W.R. commenced bus operation in the heart of deepest Wales with a twenty-mile route from Abergavenny to Brecon, using three vehicles, followed by a service from Lampeter to Aberayron (thirteen miles) on 1 October 1906. However, the G.W.R. were not the first railway operator to use motorbuses for feeder services according to Charles E. Lee, who quotes the case of the narrow-gauge Lynton & Barnstaple Railway, which actually sold to the G.W.R. its very first motorbuses (*The Early Motor Bus* p. 20).

Gradually it became necessary to control the activities of buses, especially in London. Some of this was imposed by the operators themselves. For example as from 1881 they began to insist that conductors give tickets for fares received and be accountable for these. Until that time the employer required anything from 26s. to 30s. per day from a conductor, who could pocket the remainder of his often inflated takings. Even ten years later drivers and conductors threatened to come out on strike, because their employers were insisting on this rule being strictly adhered to. In that year the famous Bell Punch Company began to make its ticket punches, and to supply paste board tickets to accompany these machines.

In 1906 the Commissioner of Police for the Metropolis issued Regulation No. 12, which stated that 'All omnibuses must be so geared that their normal highest speed shall not be in excess of the maximum laid down in the Local Government Board Order, viz. 12 miles an hour.' By the following spring the Police were busy examining and testing each new London bus on Wimbledon Common before it was placed into service. They were strict, too, and in March 1907 they rejected four out of ten new Straker-Squires delivered to the L.R.C.C. However, the most comprehensive regulations were yet to come. In September 1909 they issued the 'Metropolitan Stage (Motor) Carriage Conditions for Obtaining a Certificate of Fitness for Motor Omnibuses'. Not more than sixteen top-deck and eighteen lower-deck passengers were to be carried – a requirement which fossilised for a generation the London double-decker's capacity at 34. The unladen weight was not to exceed $3\frac{1}{2}$ tons, nor the laden weight 6 tons. As far as the L.G.O.C. were concerned this speeded up their programme of replacing their mixed bag of makes with their own design of Walthamstow-built 'X' and 'B' class buses. The maximum overall chassis length was fixed at 20 ft (plus an additional 3 ft for a platform), whilst the similar measurement for the wheelbase was 14 ft 6 in. Maximum dimensions of the actual body were determined as 23 ft long by 7 ft 2 in. wide. Lower saloon seats had to be of the garden seat variety and not longitudinal, as they had been for the previous eight decades. Furthermore, no canopy could be placed on the top deck, thus sentencing Londoners to wet and windy rides until well into the 1920s.

One concern of operators, passengers and authorities alike was the prevention of so-called 'side-slip'. In February 1907 the A.C. Side-Slip Prevention Trials took place in Barlby Road, West Kensington. Six devices were tried out, namely:

(i) loose metal ring (Messrs. W. Sully & P. H. Shailer)
(ii) floating metal ring (George B. Winter)
(iii) six-wheeled device (H. B. Molesworth)
(iv) K.T. tyre with rubber studs (J. Liversidge & Son)
(v) rubber tyre block (Hartridge Tire Syndicate)
(vi) leather tyre and rubber rings (Westminster Industrial & Finance Developments)

As the reporter of *The Commercial Motor* recorded, Mr. Molesworth's six wheels 'demonstrated, very clearly, its capability of running, in a physically straight line, over the appalling surface mud laid down for these trials'. Yet it was to be another twenty years before the six-wheeler double-decker made its regular début on the streets of London.

Meanwhile the fate of the horse bus was being slowly but surely sealed. Our Dumb Friends League put up notices inside buses that read 'Stop the Bus as Seldom as Possible, as Restarting is a Great Strain Upon the Horses'. Indeed the life of a bus horse was reckoned to be four to five years. Then, if he had not dropped dead, he was sold for lighter duties, or else to the notorious knackers. H. Thomson Lyon (Chairman of the Westminster City Council Highways Committee) in May 1909 called for 'horseless Sundays' in considerable areas of London. In fact he set up a Horseless Sunday Committee, but this body was unable to come to a satisfactory agreement with the L.G.O.C. Nevertheless, in the first issue of *The Commercial Motor* for 1911 'One Hears' wrote 'That "horseless Sunday" in London has already become almost a commonplace.'

Vehicle registration numbers had been carried by all motor/electric-battery buses since 1904, and by the end of 1906 the larger London operators were booking blocks of these. Thus the L.M.O.C. took A 9101 –9200 and LC 5001–5100, whilst the London & District Motor Bus Company and the London & Provincial Motor Bus & Traction Company (alias 'Arrow') held LC 2200–2249 and LC 3800 onwards. Because certain licensing authorities such as Brighton, West Sussex and Wiltshire would not do this, the operators, with Douglas MacKenzie in their ranks, resorted to obtaining blocks of County Armagh registrations. Hence we find Wilts. & Dorset using IB 801–6 and Worthing Motor Services employing IB 701–10. When a vehicle was sold the number was re-used on its replacement. Thus A 9118 was first seen on an L.M.O.C. Wolseley, and later on its replacement, a Milnes-Daimler. When a vehicle was lent out on trials it might also be re-registered, as happened in the case of Thornycroft H 1936, which became O 1279 while on tests in Birmingham. West Bromwich used EA 300–303 for a quartet of Albion A12s in 1914, and when the bodies from these vehicles were placed on some new Edisons in the following year the registrations were transferred too – so saving a bit of paint fore and aft! The G.W.R. used the nearest local licensing authority for the route on which a particular bus was to work. Thus they had Milnes-Daimlers registered EJ 37 (Herefordshire), AF 80 (Cornwall), T 490 (Devon) and LC 1172 (London). Other buses received their registrations from the licensing authority in whose area they had been built. So we find Leylands (Lancashire) registered B 2113 with the Stafford Motor Services & Supply, and B 2223/4 and B 2242 with Autocar of Tunbridge Wells (Kent). Likewise Commers' (Bedfordshire) BM 1605 was sold to an operator in Littlehampton and BM 1606 to another in Ireland. The same tended to be the case with the Coventry firms of Daimler and Maudslay (DU registrations). To Potteries Electric Traction belongs the unique honour of having one of their vehicles bear the very first number issued by a licensing authority: EH 1 (of Stoke-on-Trent). Already by 1906 larger operators were also reserving blocks of fleet numbers for vehicles. The L.G.O.C. used 01 to 099 for their Milnes-Daimlers; 100–199 for Straker-Squires; 200–299 for De Dion-Boutons; 300–399 for Wolseleys; 400–499 for Clarksons. On the other hand the Great Eastern London used Nos. 1–111 for horse buses, and then came a compromise No. 112 (a Büssing with a cut down horse bus body for learner duties), followed by new motorbuses consecutively from No. 113.

Around 1907 a new type of public road transport was being tried out in this country, namely the Renard Train. An advertisement claimed that the 'train' was made up of 'three to six followers. Each driven, not trailed'. 12 m.p.h. was boasted of, and up to 50 passengers together with 3 to 4 tons of luggage carried in one such 'train'. Although this idea did catch on to a limited extent on the Continent, it never had any real success in Britain.

The new form of transport that was a success towards the close of our period was the trolleybus. As J. Joyce states in his *The Story of Passenger Transport in Britain* (p. 148), 'Most people at first were rather half-hearted about the "trackless". Like most compromises, it was accepted without enthusiasm. It was regarded as little more than a poor relation of the tram, to be employed only where you could not afford the real thing.' It is amazing to think that it was as long ago as 29 April 1882 that Werner von Siemens built and ran the world's first trolleybus in the Halensee district of Berlin. It was 26 years later that the first plans for a trolleybus system in Britain were drawn up. In November 1908 Messrs. Dodd & Dodd of Birmingham announced plans to install trolleybuses in Malvern, Worcs. The following week from north of the border came the news that the Dalkeith Railless Electric Car Company had been formed to operate six 34-seat trolleybuses between Edinburgh and Dalkeith on a ten-minute headway. By December that year Middlesbrough Corporation was discussing the possibility of starting trolleybus routes, whilst Oldham and Salford were both adding 'trolley omnibus' clauses to private transport bills soon to be presented in Parliament. However, it was at the Hendon depot of M.E.T. that the first actual British trials were staged in September 1909. By then there were 60 route-miles being operated on the Filovia system in Italy, whilst trolleybuses were also successfully working on the streets of Vienna and Mulhaussen.

It was on 24 June 1911 that the general public could for the first time ride on trolleybuses on regular routes in Britain, when services commenced simultaneously in Bradford and Leeds. By that time all the above-mentioned earlier schemes had fallen by the wayside. The first leader in the *Financial Times* for 14 August 1911 had an article on 'what is known as railless electric traction or the trolley omnibus'. The writer commented on the current situation in the following terms: 'Tramway enterprise in Great Britain is practically at a standstill. Owing to various causes – notably the influence of legislation and of municipal action – the return upon tramway capital had been disappointing.' The article went on to make some observations on the likely future pattern of trolleybus expansion in Britain, making these points:—

(i) trolleys will undertake feeder duties for tram routes.
(ii) Sheffield is planning to try out trolleys on some routes, prior to converting these routes to tramway operation.
(iii) small tramless towns (e.g. Bedford, Watford) could adopt trolleys.
(iv) trolleys were ideal for steering round parked traffic in narrow streets (Edinburgh is considering them from this vantage point)

Of the eight trackless trolley schemes mooted in December 1910, only those of Aberdare and Rotherham actually commenced working; the others (Chiswick U.D.C., Halifax, Newcastle, Northampton, Lancashire Tramways Company and Brighton) did not materialise, although four of these did at a later date start such systems. Of a similar list two years later, only those at Mexborough and Swinton and in the Rhondda came to anything, Huddersfield, Derby and Chesterfield having to wait a number of years more, whilst Folkestone, Southport and West Bromwich never did get their trolleybuses. Even when trolleybuses did begin operating, the local press either ignored them (as in the case of the *Dundee Advertiser*), or else insisted on calling them 'trams' (as with both the *Aberdare Leader* and the *Ramsbottom Observer*).

By 1917 there were eight trolleybus systems operating, with two for differing reasons having already packed up (namely Dundee and the Rhondda). The total of trolleybuses licensed (but not yet bearing registration numbers) was 52, with a further eight in store awaiting service with the planned networks in Halifax and Teesside that became operational after our period.

1917 also saw the demise of the first British electric tramway system. This was the one at Sheerness, which had started as an electrified network in 1903. Two years prior to this the horse tramway of Warrenpoint and Rostrevor in Ireland (started 1877) had closed down. Two more came to an end in 1919, namely Galway and Salthill (dating from 1879) and the City of Derry (1897).

Just as the Great Exhibition had given a tremendous boost to the knifeboard horse bus, so the Coronation of King George V in June 1911 did the same for the motorbus. Whereas when his father Edward VII had gone to Westminster Abbey there were only twenty motorbuses on the capital's streets, nine years later they amounted to 1,500. Some L.G.O.C. motorbus routes ran a two-minute headway to cope with tourists, whilst they also staged sixpenny 'Decorations Trips'.

An editorial in *The Commercial Motor* for 18 April 1912 sums up the advances in motorbus design over the previous six years in these words: 'The modern motorbus is "noiseless" compared with that of 1906, when it habitually travelled in a series of jumps, partly by reason of clutch deficiencies, partly by reason of gearing deficiencies, and partly by reason of ignition deficiencies.' In the earlier issue of 3 August 1911 he had remarked that 'improvements in body construction, including the more general use of flush-sided bodies of the so-called torpedo type, will be much appreciated'.

Nor must we forget the development of the motor-coach or charabanc. From the popular horse drawn waggonette and charabanc, there had evolved a powerful vehicle that was a far cry from the 12-h.p. Daimler waggonette that Barton had used to take his trippers from Weston-super-Mare to Cheddar Gorge in 1903. Eight years later *The Commercial Motor* printed the weekly schedule of three Leyland 35/40-h.p. charabancs named 'King George', 'Queen Mary' and 'Prince Edward', which were used for Bolton Wanderer's matches, when not engaged on the following exacting programme:—

| Sunday | to Ilkley (95 miles) |
| Monday | to Morecambe (90 miles) |

Tuesday	to Blackpool (80 miles)
Wednesday	OVERHAUL
Thursday	to Grasmere (155 miles)
Friday	to Blackpool (80 miles)
Saturday	to Southport, twice (125 miles)
	Grand total for week = 625 miles

In 1913 Bath Electric Tramways ran a six-day charabanc tour covering 170 miles in the following stages: Bath to Brecon (Mons.), Brecon to Barmouth (Tues.), Barmouth to Llandudno (Weds.), Llandudno to Dolgelly (Thurs.), Dolgelly to Shrewsbury (Fris.), Shrewsbury to Bath (Sats.).

In the autumn of 1908 the Commanding Officer of the 5th Battn. Essex Regt. (T.A.) hired two Clarkson steamers to transport his men between Chelmsford and Shoeburyness. This so impressed the War Office that on 18 December that year they borrowed 24 L.G.O.C. Strakers and De Dions, along with some L.M.O.C. Milnes-Daimlers, to carry 500 troops and their equipment. These were the first steps in the procession that eventually led in the First World War to hundreds of A.EC.-L.G.O.C. 'B' class buses finding their way across the Channel. to the battlefields of Flanders.

The success of the motorbus had resulted in a reduction of fares by 1911. The L.G.O.C. introduced ½d. fares on their Marble Arch to Cricklewood route in December of that year, and this was shortly followed by other similar reductions. The longest ½d. fare in London appeared to be between Canning Town Station and Green Street (a distance of 2,202 yards!). This compared with the longest 1d. stage of Birch Grove to Uxbridge Road Station (a distance of 5,204 yards). The longest London route at this juncture was service 8 (Willesden to Seven Kings). For the 17·55 miles passengers paid a fare of 6d. from one terminus to the other. At the same time, passenger journeys on L.G.O.C. buses had gone up from 145 per head of population per annum in London in 1903 to 238 per head in 1912.

A LIST OF SOME OF THE TITLES USED FOR STAGE COACHES

A name within brackets denotes the town on which a coach was based. Several names within brackets indicates that there were coaches of the same name based on several towns.

1. Aberdeen, Earl of (Strichen)
2. Accommodation (Daventry, Lincoln, Worthing)
3. Age (Brighton, Bristol, Oxford, Tunbridge Wells)
4. Albion (Liverpool)
5. Alert (Brighton, Oxford)
6. Alpha (Southampton)
7. Annihilator (Great Yarmouth)
8. Antiquary (Edinburgh)
9. Aurora (Kirkcaldy)
10. Balcarras (Anstruther, Kinross)
11. Balloon (Liverpool, Manchester)
12. Banks o' Dee (Banchory)
13. Banks o' Don (Inverurie)
14. Banks o' Ythan (Old Deer)
15. Beaufort (Brighton)
16. Beauty, Queen of (Perth)
17. Bedford Times (Bedford)
18. Beehive (Cambridge, Manchester)
19. Berkeley Hunt (Cheltenham)
20. Blenheim (Oxford)
21. Blue (Wickham Market)
22. Brighton Day Mail (Brighton)
23. Britannia (Kilmarnock)
24. British Queen (Maidstone)
25. Bury Fly (Bury)
26. Caledonian (Edinburgh, Fort William, Inverness, Wick)
27. Cambrian (Wales)
28. Carron (Edinburgh)
29. Champion (Hereford)
30. Chevy Chase (Glasgow)
31. Chronometer (Exeter)
32. Cobourg (Brighton, Manchester)
33. Comet (Bognor, Brighton, Littlehampton, Southampton)
34. Commerce, Sons of (Gravesend)
35. Commercial (Glasgow, Nottingham)
36. Commercial Traveller (Arbroath)
37. Commodore (Brampton, Liverpool)
38. Cornwallis, Marquis of (Bury St. Edmunds)
39. Criterion (Chester)
40. Crown Prince (Brighton, Elstree)
41. Dart (Brighton, Dartford)
42. Defiance (Aberdeen, Exeter, Fife, Fraserburgh, Glasgow, Inverness, Manchester, Oxford, Stamford, Tain, Thurso, Wisbech)
43. Delight (Chester)
44. Despatch (Aylesbury, Hastings, Southend)
45. Diligence (Edinburgh)
46. Diligent (Mousehill)
47. Dilly (Edinburgh)
48. Drake (Plymouth)
49. Eagle (Canterbury, Glasgow)
50. Eclipse (Brighton, Colchester, Hertford, Southampton)
51. Economist (Birmingham)
52. Emerald (Brighton, Bristol, Hoddesdon)
53. Enterprise (Wisbech)
54. Erin-go-Bragh (Dublin)
55. Estafette (Manchester)
56. Express (Aberdeen, Barton-on-Humber, Bristol, Dover, Gosport, Hastings, Hertford, Leeds, Liverpool)
57. Fair Maid (Dundee)
58. Fair Play (Great Yarmouth)
59. Favourite (Haddington, Maidstone)
60. Fife, Earl of (Banff)
61. Fly (Cambridge, Coggeshall, Dunfermline, Glasgow, Haddington, Perth)
62. Forbes, Lord (Strathdon)

63. Forest Coach (Reading)
64. Forth & Clyde (Edinburgh)
65. Frobisher (Plymouth)
66. Give & Take (Hastings)
67. Glenury (Stonehaven)
68. Good Intent (Haddington, High Wycombe)
69. Grey, Earl (Dunbar)
70. Greyhound (Birmingham, Shrewsbury)
71. Harkaway (Birmingham)
72. Herald (Exeter)
73. Hero (Hastings, Moffatt, Portsmouth, Worthing)
74. High Flyer (Edinburgh, Glasgow, Holyhead, York)
75. Highland Chieftain (Dunfermline)
76. Highlander (Montrose)
77. Highland Lass (Inverurie)
78. Hirondelle (Cheltenham)
79. Hope, The (Newark)
80. Howieson, John (Edinburgh)
81. Independent (Carlisle, Chichester, Edinburgh, Glasgow, Portsmouth, Southampton, Tunbridge Wells)
82. Independent New Post (Hastings)
83. Independent Safe (Southampton)
84. Independent Tally-Ho! (Birmingham)
85. Industry (Luton)
86. Ipswich Blue (Ipswich)
87. Item (Brighton)
88. Kershaw's Coach (Welwyn)
89. Kershaw's Safety Coach (Hitchin)
90. Kingdom of Fife (Dundee)
91. Land Frigate (Portsmouth)
92. Lewes (Fyvie)
93. Life Preserver (Great Yarmouth)
94. Light Salisbury (Salisbury)
95. Live-and-Let-Live (Southend)
96. Loch Leven Castle (Kinross)
97. Magnet (Brighton, Cheltenham, Norwich, Weymouth)
98. Mar, Earl of (Stirling)
99. Marlow Coach, The Original (Marlow)
100. Martin's (Maidstone)
101. Matcham's Coach (Reading)

102. Mazeppa (Oxford)
103. Monarch (Bristol)
104. Monarch of the East (Dunbar)
105. Morning Star (Tunbridge Wells)
106. Nelson (Brompton, Portsmouth)
107. New (Colchester)
108. New Dart (Brighton)
109. New Post Coach (Reading)
110. New Reform (Newcastle)
111. New Times (Aberdeen)
112. Nimrod (Birmingham, Shrewsbury)
113. Norfolk Hero (Wells-next-the-Sea)
114. North Briton (Liverpool)
115. North Devon Telegraph (Taunton)
116. No Wonder (Dunkeld)
117. Old Bury (Bury St. Edmunds)
118. Old Salisbury (Salisbury)
119. Owen Glendower (Wales)
120. Oxonian (Oxford)
121. Paragon (Hastings)
122. Parnell, Sir Henry (Brechin)
123. Paul Pry (Worcester)
124. Perseverance (Boston, Glasgow, Horndon)
125. Peveril of the Peak (Manchester)
126. Phenomena (Norwich)
127. Phoenix (Dover)
128. Pilot (Dunbarton, Hemel Hempstead, Worthing)
129. Prince Regent (Brighton)
130. Quicksilver (Brighton, Southampton)
131. Red Rover (Bristol, Liverpool, Manchester, Southampton)
132. Regent (Brighton, Stamford)
133. Regulator (Brighton, Bristol, Gloucester, Hastings, Holt, Oundle, Portsmouth)
134. Reliance (Maidstone)
135. Retaliator (Glasgow, Gloucester, Hertford, Oxford)
136. Richmond, Duke of (Chichester)
137. Rival (Cheltenham)
138. Rob Roy (Loch Goilhead)
139. Rocket (Cambridge, Hertford, Portsmouth)
140. Rockingham (Leeds)
141. Rodway's Coach (Hemel Hempstead)

142. Royal Blue (Brighton, Hastings, Portsmouth)
143. Royal Bruce (Glasgow, Manchester)
144. Royal Brunswick (Brighton)
145. Royal Charlotte (Edinburgh)
146. Royal Clarence (Brighton)
147. Royal Defiance (Manchester)
148. Royal Express (York)
149. Royal Forester (Gloucester)
150. Royal George (Brighton)
151. Royal Liverpool (Liverpool)
152. Royal Oak (Greenock)
153. Royal Sovereign (Brighton)
154. Royal Sussex (Brighton, Little-hampton)
155. Royal Union (Dundee)
156. Royal Victoria (Brighton)
157. Royal William (Southampton)
158. Salopian (Shrewsbury)
159. Saxe-Coburg (Perth)
160. Shannon (Yoxford)
161. Southampton Times (Southampton)
162. Sovereign (Braintree, Brighton, Hastings, Leamington, Rye, Worcester, Worthing)
163. Stag (Peebles, Shrewsbury)
164. Star (Cambridge, Horsham)
165. Star of Brunswick (Portsmouth)
166. Strathmore Union (Aberdeen)
167. Sudbury, New (Sudbury)
168. Sussex (Tunbridge Wells)
169. Swift (Montrose)
170. Swiftsure (Bridgwater)
171. Tally-Ho! (Birmingham, Canterbury, Dundee, Huntly, Stirling, Tenterden)
172. Tantivy (Birmingham, Faversham)
173. Telegraph (Ayr, Billericay, Bishops Stortford, Brighton, Cambridge, Dover, Exeter, Haverhill, Maldon, Manchester, Norwich, Reading, Southampton, Southend, Tunbridge Wells, Worcester, Worthing)
174. Thame Safety Coach (Thame)
175. Times (Brighton, Cambridge, Dover, Folkestone, Guildford, Luton, Norwich, Portsmouth, Sunbridge)
176. Tollitt's Coach (Uxbridge)
177. Trafalgar (Portsmouth)
178. Traveller (Exeter)
179. True Blue (Brighton, Portsmouth)
180. True Briton (Glasgow, Leeds)
181. Tweedside (Edinburgh)
182. Umpire (Liverpool)
183. Union (Banbury, Birmingham, Blackwater, Brighton, Dover, Guildford, King's Lynn, Leeds, Leicester, Nairn, Tunbridge Wells, Windsor)
184. United Friends (Sevenoaks)
185. Vivid (Brighton)
186. Wales, Prince of (Worthing)
187. Waterloo (Perth)
188. Wellington (Colchester)
189. Wellington, Duke of (Inverness)
190. Wellington, Lord (Newcastle)
191. White Hart (Bath)
192. Wisbech Day Coach (Wisbech)
193. Wonder (Nottingham, Shrewsbury)
194. Yarmouth Star (Great Yarmouth)
195. York House (Bath, Brighton)

FLEET NAMES OF SOME LONDON MOTORBUS OPERATORS
BEFORE 1919

ARROW	{ London & District Motor Bus Co. Ltd.
	{ London & Provincial Motor Bus & Traction Co. Ltd.
ASSOCIATED	Associated Omnibus Co. Ltd.
BRITISH.	British Automobile Traction Co. Ltd.
CENTRAL	{ London Central Motor Omnibus Co. Ltd.
	{ New Central Omnibus Co. Ltd.
ELECTROBUS	London Electrobus Co. Ltd.
GEARLESS	Gearless Motor Omnibus Co. Ltd.
GENERAL	London General Omnibus Co. Ltd.
GREAT EASTERN. . .	Great Eastern London Motor Omnibus Co. Ltd.
KINGSWAY . . .	New London & Suburban Omnibus Co. Ltd.
NATIONAL	National Steam Car Co. Ltd.
OLD VIC	Victoria Omnibus Co. Ltd.
PARAGON	Balls Bros.
PILOT	Motor Bus Co. Ltd.
PIONEER	London Power Omnibus Co. Ltd.
PREMIER	London Premier Omnibus Co. Ltd.
RAPIDE	Rapid Road Transit Co. Ltd.
UNION JACK . . .	London Road-Car Co. Ltd.
VANGUARD . . .	{ London Motor Omnibus Co. Ltd.
	{ Vanguard Motorbus Co. Ltd.

HORSE BUSES IN LONDON (1834–92)

1834	376
1839	620
1850	almost 1,300
1854	1,160
1856	810
1892	2,210

METROPOLITAN RECORDS OF BUSES IN LONDON (1897–1912)

Year	Motorbuses	Horse Buses	Grand Total
1897	1	3,190	3,191
1898	nil	3,423	3,423
1899	5	3,621	3,626
1900	4	3,681	3,685
1901	10	3,736	3,746
1902	29	3,667	3,696
1903	13	3,623	3,636
1904	31	3,551	3,582
1905	241	3,484	3,725
1906	783	2,964	3,747
1907	1,205	2,557	3,762
1908	1,133	2,155	3,288
1909	1,180	1,771	2,951
1910	1,200	1,103	2,303
1911	1,962	786	2,748
1912	2,908	376	3,284

In the descriptive text and plates that now follow, the vehicles described have been split up for the readers' convenience into five categories, viz.

Section I: Horse-drawn vehicles (chronologically)
Section II: Steamers (chronologically)
Section III: Electric vehicles (alphabetically)
Section IV: Petrol and petrol-electric vehicles, 1898–1909 (alphabetically)
Section V: Petrol and petrol-electric vehicles, 1910–1919 (alphabetically)

ERRATUM

The captions to colour illustrations 1 and 3 are unfortunately transposed.

1 This Northampton to London **stage coach** spent some years on display outside Chessington Zoo.

2 A large **stage coach** built by the London firm of **Holland & Holland** c. 1840 for the Walker-Morrison family of Fife. Now it is in Glasgow's Transport Museum.

3 Seen at the 1971 Fosseway Traction Engine Rally near Newark, this **stage coach** ran originally between London and Cardiff. It was built by **Holland & Holland** c. 1837.

4 A **Royal Mail** coach of c. 1820, which is preserved at the Science Museum at South Kensington.

5   The famous **Royal Mail** coach 'Quicksilver', which
    used to cover the 176 miles from London to Exeter
    in 17½ hours. Now it is in the Hull Transport
    Museum.

6   This model of **Shillibeer's 1829 Omnibus** shows
    very clearly the rear entrance into the 22-seat saloon.

7   This full-size replica of **Shillibeer's** original three-horse **Omnibus** is at present kept by the Museum of British Transport at Clapham.

8   Thomas Tilling introduced this **knifeboard** between Camberwell and Oxford Street about 1851. It held 24 passengers.

9 A Science Museum model of a typical London **knifeboard** double-decker of 1855.

10 The Richmond Conveyance Company operated this **'Improved' omnibus** in 1860. It carried twelve passengers inside and thirteen on the roof.

11 Hibernia Company **knifeboard** No. 7 stands outside Fortwilliam Park, Belfast c. 1870.

12 Nottingham & District Tramways Company ran this **knifeboard** between Basford and Burwell in 1878.

13 Note the small front wheels of this twin forward-staircase experimental London Road Car Company bus of 1881.

14 The L.G.O.C. operated this small **one-horse bus,** known as 'First Bumper', on their Highbury Station to Highbury Barns route in the 1880s.

15 T. Howe of Gateshead operated this **one-horse** 30-
seat single-decker over the High Level Bridge at
Newcastle upon Tyne until 1931.

16 A **garden seat** horse bus standing beside a Guernsey Railways steam tram at St. Peter Port.

17 A **garden seat** bus operated by South Shields
Tramways Company.

18 A 24-seat **garden seat** bus that was placed in service
by the L.G.O.C. in 1886, which has found a place in
the Museum of British Transport at Clapham.

19 Formerly with the Star Omnibus Company of London, this two-horse **garden seat** bus ran between Chessington South railway station and Chessington Zoo from 1944 until 1948.

20 **Hendersons** of Glasgow built this 10-seater **station bus** for Lawsons to use on their Kirkintilloch route. It is now in the Glasgow Transport Museum.

21 This **station bus** is now part of the Shuttleworth
collection at Old Warden Aerodrome, Beds.

22 An 1895 **two-horse waggonette,** which was used
for taking people to the Beverley Races until 1922,
and is now in the Hull Transport Museum.

23 A Science Museum model of an 1890 **charabanc** seating 22, such as was used by Chapman & Sons of Queen's Mews, London.

24 The Ardrishaig Belle, a large **horse charabanc** used for excursions, now on view at the Glasgow Transport Museum.

25 A **two-horse charabanc** owned by Paragon of Jersey, seen here at Royal Bay c. 1910.

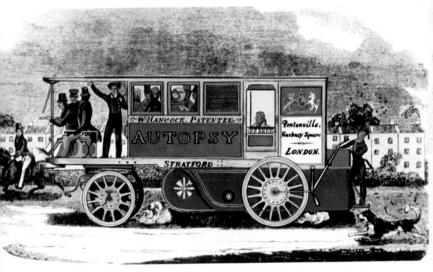

26 **Walter Hancock** experimented with this steam carriage, **'Autopsy'**, in London during 1833/4.

27 **Hancock's** larger **'Automaton',** which appeared in 1836 and sat 22. Note the brake boy at the rear.

28 Five-inch indiarubber tyres were fitted to this **Thomson steam tractor and trailer** that ran between Edinburgh and Leith in 1870.

29 London General's first motorbus to enter *regular* service was this **Clarkson steamer** in October 1904.

30 LC 8630, one of the 1906 batch of **Clarkson Chelmsfords** purchased by the L.G.O.C.

31 The National Steam Car Company ran many **Clarkson Chelmsfords** like F 4801 on their central London routes in Edwardian times.

32 The Harrogate Road Car Company's **Clarkson Chelmsford** C 5919, seen taking on water at Starbeck Station c. 1910.

33   The Motor Omnibus Syndicate ran this **Gillette steam lorry** chassis bus with a 24-seat double-deck body on trials in the London area in January 1899.

34 The L.R.C.C. **Thornycroft steambus** that ran between Hammersmith and Oxford Circus during the spring of 1902. Note the horse bus body.

35 **Trolleybus** 503, which **Bradford Corporation** built for itself, installing two Siemens electric motors.

36   For a short while at the end of 1914 Rhondda Tramways operated **Brush-Cleveland trolleybus** No.
58 on their Williamstown to Gilfach Goch route.

37 A **Brush trolleybus** powered by a Cedes-Stoll motor, one of a trio bought by Stockport Corporation. Stockport adopted the Lloyd-Kohler system of current collection.

38 Keighley Corporation's No. 0, one of the first **Cedes-Stoll trolleybuses** to be operated in Britain.

39 Aberdare U.D.C. employed this **Cedes-Stoll trolleybus** with 27-seat Dodson bodywork.

40 Although **Daimlers** produced very few **trolley-buses,** they were one of the first into the field. This is one of three built for Mexborough & Swinton Traction in 1915.

41 Lancaster Corporation Nos. 1 (B 5981) and 2
(B 5979): **Edison battery** buses with Brush bodywork.

42 Steps projected in front of Lancaster's No. 4 (B 5998),
another **Edison** with a locally built Hardy body. It
stands by the recharging box.

43 Derby Corporation's No. 2 (CH 1812), an **Edison**
purchased just after the Armistice in 1918.

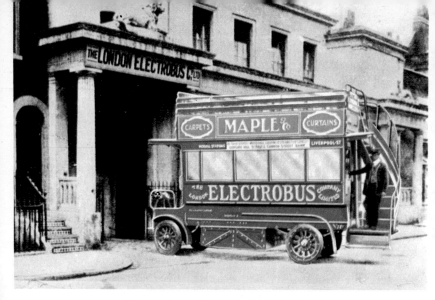

44 A 1907 vintage **Electrobus,** entering the Earl Street Depot (off Great Smith Street) for battery recharging.

45 Bradford Corporation's first trolleybus, No. 240, a **Railless Electric Traction** with a Milnes body, seen here at Thornbury Depot in 1911, its first year.

46 Sister trolleybus No. 241, who ended her days as battery waggon No. 502.

47 Leeds Corporation also started trolleybus operation in June 1911 with four **R.E.Ts,** including No. 501, featured here with No. 505 of 1915 vintage.

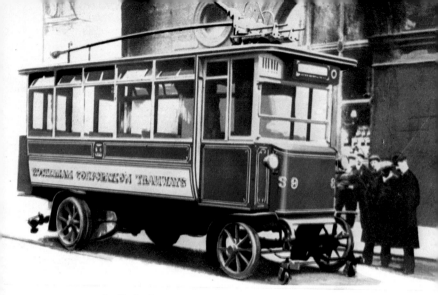

48 Rotherham Corporation No. 39, one of three **R.E.Ts** bought to start its trolleybus network in 1912.

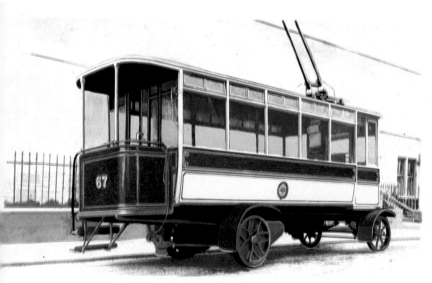

49 Dundee No. 67, one of a pair of **R.E.Ts** tried out between 1912 and 1914. Later it passed into the hands of Halifax Corporation. Note the open platform.

50 One of a trio of **Railless trolleybuses,** which had
the unusual Schiemann system of current collection,
purchased by Ramsbottom U.D.C. in 1913.

51 MN 68, a 1907 **35 h.p. Argus** belonging to the
Manx Electric Railway Company, who used it on a
feeder route to Sulby Glen. Here it is seen at
Bungalow.

52   The Great Eastern London Motor Omnibus Company used this **Arrol Johnston** (AN 653) on one of their East End routes.

53   Guernsey Railway's No. 3 (A 82) with an Andrews 34-seat body, one of three 1906 vintage **Brillié-Schneiders** bought from the Star Bus Company of London. Note the driver sitting above the engine.

54 LC 6309, a **Brush** belonging to the Amalgamated Motor Bus Company. Note the 'decency' boards fitted to the fancy wrought ironwork grille.

55 EC 634, an 11-seater **Commer** of 1909. It spent its life in the service of Lord Lonsdale, and is now preserved.

56   This early **motor waggonette** of unknown make, used by Watson & Co. of Liverpool on an experimental route to Chester, stands outside the G.W.R. office in Wrexham c. 1901.

57   EE 313, a 1906 **Dennis** which originated as a one man operated bus with Mail Motor, before passing into the Provincial ranks. Note the front nearside stairs.

58 This 1905 vintage **De Dion-Bouton** of London General was among the first of a large number of these French buses to grace the streets of Edwardian London.

59 W 2193, a **Durham-Churchill** charabanc owned by Rhyl & Potteries, seen on Rhyl seafront.

60   Barton's original No. 1 (W 963), a 20-seater **Durham-Churchill,** off to Goose Fair, Nottingham in 1908.

61   In 1963 Bartons built this replica of No. 1, using a **Daimler CB** chassis. Note the difference in the wheels of the two versions.

62   This **Fischer petrol-electric** bus was imported from the U.S.A. in 1903 by the L.G.O.C. for their first experiments in motorbus operation.

63   The driver sat immediately above the engine in this **Germain** operated by the L.R.C.C. Note the flag pole for the Union Jack, the company's patriotic insignia.

64 The **Great Eastern Railway** built its own buses
at the beginning of this century. A typical one is
BJ 416, which ran on their Lowestoft to Southwold
route.

65 **Hallford** of Dartford and **Stevens** of Maidstone
combined forces to build this **petrol-electric bus**
for Thomas Tillings to operate in 1908.

66 Between 1902 and 1904 this unwieldy **Cannstatt-Daimler** ran on rubber tyres from Lewisham to Eltham.

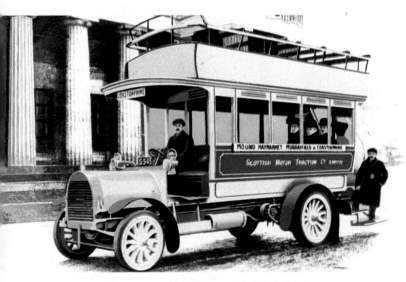

67 No. 51 (S 543), S.M.T's first Edinburgh-based motorbus, a 35-seat **Maudslay** which commenced work on New Year's Day, 1906.

68 S 1378, an S.M.T. **Maudslay charabanc,** seen on
Waverley Bridge, Edinburgh c. 1912.

69 IJ 159, an early **Maudslay** bus operated in County
Down.

70 DY 84, the 1904 prototype **Milnes-Daimler 24 h.p.,** which was run by the Hastings & St. Leonard's Omnibus Company on a route from the Kite's Nest to West Marina.

71 This **Milnes-Daimler 24 h.p.** (A 6934) was the first motorbus operated by Thomas Tillings in London in 1904.

72   The L.M.O.C. employed this **Milnes-Daimler 24 h.p.** on its Wormwood Scrubs to Herne Hill route.

73   Worthing Motor Omnibus Company's 1905 **Milnes-Daimler,** BP 311, at the West Tarring terminus.

74 LC 2370, a **Moss & Woodd 'Orion'** bought by the Victoria Omnibus Company in 1905.

75 Leeds Corporation's first two motorbuses, U 327/8, a pair of 1905 vintage **Ryknield-Belsizes** with Corporation-built 34-seat bodies.

76 Bournemouth Corporation's first motorbus was this 1906 **Straker-McConnell,** seen here at the South-cote Road Depot.

77 L.G.O.C.'s No. P37 (LN 4552), an example of the popular **Straker-Squire-Büssing** double-decker, so many of which were used in Edwardian London.

78 CE 4031, a **Straker-Squire** used by Ortona of Cambridge on their local route 6.

79 AE 723, one of a batch of **Thornycroft Type 80** double-deckers purchased in 1906 by the Bristol Tram & Carriage Company.

80 The leading all-British built bus on the streets of
London in 1908 was the **Wolseley 24 h.p.,** of which
London General's LN 4502 is typical.

81 **London General's X7** of 1909. It was out of such buses that the famous A.E.C./L.G.O.C. 'B' class was evolved.

82 A queue of former **L.G.O.C. 'B' class** buses on the Cassel to Dunkerque road behind the Western Front in August 1917. Note the boarded windows.

83 An early conductress on LF 8285, one of the prolific **'B' class** of **London General**.

84 Normally No. 17 in the Chiswick Works fleet of lorries, this **A.E.C. 'B'** was brought into passenger service by the L.G.O.C. during an emergency.

85 This **A.E.C. 'B'** single-decker was No. A105 (AH 0602) in the United Automobile fleet. It had started life as a lorry.

86 EA 300/1, two of a quartet of **Albion A12s** bought by West Bromwich Corporation in 1914 to commence motorbus operations. Next year the bodies were transferred to new Edison electric chassis.

87 Walling of Eastergate, Sussex had a new Strachan & Brown body fitted to this ex-War Department **Austin 2/3 tonner** ambulance chassis.

88 Guernsey Railway Company's No. 4, an 11-seater **Clement-Bayard.**

89 Provincial No. 5 (EE 705), a **Commer CC,** here seen on an excursion at Immingham in 1911.

90   Provincial No. 6 (EE 706), a 1912 **Commer CC**
29-seat charabanc.

91   EE 706 with its later single-deck bus body, being
worked off a gas cylinder mounted on the roof.

92   BM 2856, a 15-seater **Commer WP3** charabanc,
now preserved, and once the property of Lord
Lonsdale.

93   East Surrey's P 5167, one of many **Daimler CC**
models placed into service just before the beginning
of the First World War.

94   1914 was the date of entry into service of this City of Oxford Electric Tramways Company's **Daimler CC** with an L.G.O.C. body.

95   City of Oxford No. 29 (FC 4632), another **Daimler CC,** this time with a charabanc body.

96   Birmingham Corporation's No. 48 (OB 2102) of
1916, a 33-seat Dodson bodied **Daimler Y.**

97　Great Western Railway operated this 1911 **Dennis 20 h.p.** with a company-built 13-seat body.

98 On a trial service at Horley with a woman driver,
Dennis Subsidy model P 8697, No. 7 in the fleet of
East Surrey.

99 CX 1337, an 18-seat charabanc dating from 1911,
on a **Karrier B/60** chassis.

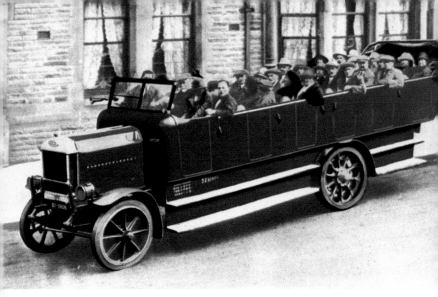

100   OI 3606, a 32-seat charabanc operated by the Laharna Hotel at Larne, County Antrim, typical of the larger **Karrier B/80.**

101   A **30 h.p. Lacre** (DM 472) of Brookes Bros., Rhyl on an excursion at Dyseth in 1912.

102   DL 493, a **Leyland X** with a 39-seat Dodson body, which was run by Worthing Motor Services on their Worthing to Storrington service, before it passed into the hands of Southdown as their No. 49.

103   Autocar of Tunbridge Wells ran this **Leyland X** on local routes in 1910.

104 Brookes Bros. **Leyland S4,** seen at Rhyl.

105 An East Surrey Traction Company **Leyland S Series** single-decker (P 7461) at Reigate.

106   Edinburgh Corporation's No. 1 (S 4440), a 29-seat
Leyland S8 of 1914 vintage which was used on the
Southern circular route.

107   Wilts. & Dorset No. 6 (IB 806), a 1916 **McCurd 40
h.p.** bearing a second-hand 26-seat clerestory body
bought from Tillings.

108　J. H. Miller of Guernsey bought this **Maxwell** as his No. 1, when he began to convert his fleet from horses in 1918.

109　Provincial No. 4 (MX 9751), a 24-seat **Napier 2 Tonner** charabanc bought from a Barnsley publican in 1913. Next to it is No. 8 (EE 758), a **40 h.p. Daimler.**

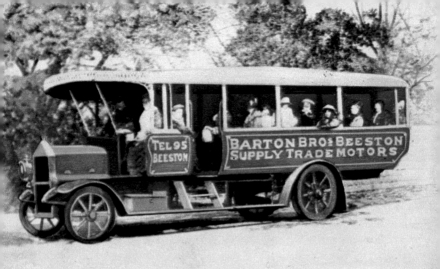

110 One of a number of **Ryknield R** chassis bought by
Bartons in 1912 and lengthened by them.

111 Note the small wheels and the curtains to keep out
the rain on this early **Scout** coach.

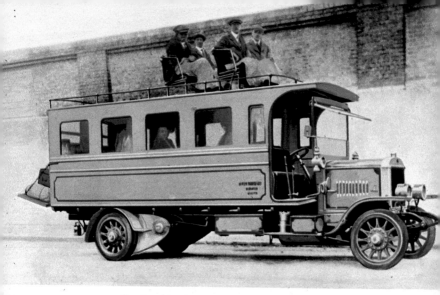

112　Roy Bartley of Handley, Dorset operated this **25 h.p. Scout** semi-pullman with its two roof seats.

113　Wilts. & Dorset's No. 4 (IB 1804), a **Scout 4 Tonner** with a 33-seat body nicknamed 'The Greenhouse', which was purchased from Worthing Motor Services.

114 Barton's **Scout** double-decker EE 1160 having its
gasbag inflated. Formerly it was in the Grimsby-
based Provincial fleet.

115 Scottish Motor Traction's No. 98 (S 4288) with 32-seat body, the ninth **Lothian** single-decker built, seen on Waverley Bridge, Edinburgh.

116 Another S.M.T. **Lothian** (No. 75, S 4770) fitted up with a gasbag during the First World War to save petrol.

117 Barton's No. 13 (AL 4408) also ran on gas at that time. This was a **Thornycroft J type** with a 36-seat Todd body.

118 The prototype **Tilling-Stevens TTA1** (LN 9998), placed into service by Thomas Tilling in 1911. Note the unusual sloping bonnet.

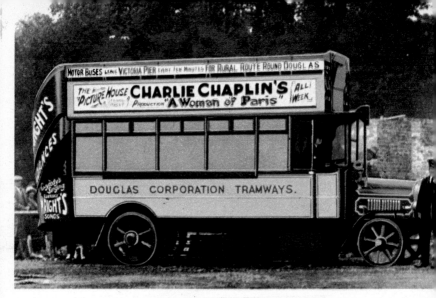

119 A **Tilling-Stevens TTA1 petrol-electric** operated by Douglas Corporation Tramways.

120 Birmingham Corporation No. 28 (O 9928) with Brush 34-seat body, an example of the **Tilling-Stevens TTA2,** seen here on the Harborne route.

SECTION I: HORSE-DRAWN VEHICLES

Coachwaggons

The successor to the medieval whirlicotes appears to have been the so-called 'Coachwaggons', such as were advertised as running out of Grantham in 1681. According to Stow in his *Annales* it was in 1564 that 'began long waggons to come in use, such as now come to London from Canterbury, Norwich, Ipswich, Gloucester &c. with passengers and commodities'. These vehicles were sometimes called 'Gee Hos'. They had first class accommodation in a leather compartment hung by chains in the middle of the waggon. They were drawn by eight horses, with an additional pair held in readiness for pulling the vehicle through sloughs and up hills. In 1576 a coach fitting this description was imported from Pomerania to London, with a set of spare wheels. The Queen's coachmaker at Smithfield raised its roof height for a cost of £8 10s., making a total cost of £50 10s. for the entire vehicle.

Although suspension is known to have been used in whirlicotes as early as the reign of Richard II, it did not become common for these coachwaggons until about 1620. In 1618 a royal proclamation forbad waggoners to use more than five horses, although in such dire spots as Lob Lane at Oxford it took up to twelve to shift these heavy vehicles. It is likely that they averaged 3½ m.p.h.

According to the 'Carriers' Cosmography' of 1637, all the coaches plying into London, with the exception of the Cambridge coach, came from within a radius of 30 miles. But by 1645, in spite of the Civil War (or perhaps because of it) these coachwaggons are listed in *The Traveller's Director* as coming to the capital from as far away as Newark (125 miles), while two years earlier *A Direction for the English Traveller* had showed them also coming from points westward of London as far afield as Wiltshire and Gloucestershire.

Another term for those who ran these waggoncoaches was 'demi-carriers'. The word 'coach' itself came from the name of the town of Kotze in Hungary.

Stage Coaches. Pl. 1–3

There seems to be some confusion as to when the first vehicle that could be accurately called a stage coach came into service. However, it is clear that by the middle of the Commonwealth period (i.e. 1655), there were such coaches plying between London and Exeter, and between London and Winchester. These were pulled by six horses. Two years later other runs exceeding the 170 miles to Exeter from the capital are listed: to Chester (182 miles), to York (196 miles), and to Newcastle upon Tyne (274 miles). In the 1681 edition of the *Present State of London* coaches are listed departing to 88 towns, and this total had increased to 180 towns by the time that the *Traveller's & Chapman's Instructor* was published in 1705.

The 17th-century version of the stage coach conveyed only inside passengers. Six of these sat on wooden benches facing one another. There was none of the padding we associate with the stage at that time. At the rear of the vehicle was a large wicker-work basket, known as the 'conveniency', in which the luggage was carried. Towards the end of the century it became quite common practice for any spare room in this structure to be taken up by passengers paying a reduced fare.

The invention of dished wheels in the latter half of the 16th century had given vehicles more lateral strength to their wheels. This kind of wheel also had the property of throwing the mud away from the coach. The outer circumference of the felloes (often at this time called 'fellies') had to be bevelled to prevent the wheel 'running on its toes'. The bearing surface of the wheel became conical instead of being cylindrical. Ash was normally employed for the manufacture of the felloes, whilst elm was used for making the naves. 'John Oak made the spoke' was a contemporary jingle that tells of the wood used for this vital part. It was so good a material that the life expectancy of a wheel, in spite of the rough nature of the highways, was 30 years. In place of tyres, there were rows of strakes. The axle itself was completely wooden throughout much of the stage coach era. The rear wheels varied in diameter from 5 ft 4 in. up to 5 ft 8 in., whilst there was a much greater spread with the front (or 'fore') wheels – between 3 ft 2 in. and 4 ft 6 in. The normal wheelbase of a stage coach was 9 ft 8 in. The floor level of the coach was usually about 4 ft above the road surface (when level!).

By the middle of the 18th century definite improvements had been made in the stage. The rigid roofed body was now suspended above the chassis (or 'carriage') by leather braces, which normally acted in conjunction with steel springs to insulate the passengers from the worst of the jolts. From 1753 'bows' (or handles) were provided for the outside passengers to cling on to, for passengers were now carried on the roofs of coaches. The following year Hosea Eastgate introduced a modernised vehicle on his London to Edinburgh route that was described as 'a genteel Two-end Glass Machine, hung on Steel Springs, exceeding light and easy'. However, its 4 sq. ft of window glass proved too brittle to stand the rough treatment received on an 800-mile round trip, and it was soon withdrawn from service. The steel springs themselves had originally been patented by Edward Knappe as long ago as 1625, and further experiments had been carried out with them by Robert Hooke and Colonel Blunt later that century. These necessitated the replacing of the curved bottom frame members ('rockers') with quarter-elliptics ('elbow springs'). The so-called 'telegraph' springs (named

after the 18th-century Telegraph coach) consisted of eight semi-elliptic springs (four at each end of the vehicle). Bird in his *Roads and Vehicles* (p. 92) describes these. 'Two springs were attached longitudinally above each axle bed, linked by inverted transverse springs which were bolted at their centres to suitable blocks or "pillows" below the bodywork.'

The assembly of the fore axle, axle irons, futchells, sway bars, hooping piece and splinter bar comprised the 'forecarriage', and the whole weight of the rest of the chassis body and its load were pulled along by the perch bolt, which sometimes gave way if the rear wheels hit an obstruction in the road.

James Hunt is credited with the invention of the expanded hoop tyre, which was placed in position when red hot, in 1769.

The Manchester 'Beehive' was fitted with spring cushions and a reading lamp (lighted with wax), whilst another Manchester coach, the 'Estafette' had an inside time-table which was illuminated at night.

Mail Coaches. Pl. 4, 5

The man behind the establishment of an efficient and fast mail coach network in Britain was John Palmer of Bath. He began his first service between Bristol and London, via Bath, in August 1784. His coach carried only four passengers, a driver and an armed guard, who sat on a locked box containing the mail. It kept to a strict schedule, and that was more than could be said for certain stage coaches at that time. One cannot better the description of one of these vehicles by Stella Margetson in her *Journey by Stages* (p. 90). 'Lighter and more elegant than a stage coach, it was painted maroon and black with scarlet wheels, and the doors were decorated with the Royal Arms. The emblems of the four orders of knighthood – the Garter, the Bath, the Thistle and St. Patrick – were picked out in colour on the upper panels of the body, and on the fore-boot where the coachman sat was the cipher of the reigning coachman.'

By 1790 Vidler of Millbank had the monopoly of building these vehicles. He also had the task of cleaning, greasing and overhauling them after every journey. Various improvements in coach design benefited the mail coaches especially. For example, in 1804 Obadiah Elliot of Lambeth mounted bodies of four wheeled carriages directly on elliptical springs attached to the axles, thus dispensing with the perch and cross-beds. Fourteen years later Windus of Bishopgate Street invented an 'under-spring' perch carriage, and this was developed by Samuel Hobson of Long Acre.

As regards strengthening the axles, John Besant's 'Mail' box of 1795 was a distinct advance in this field. Made of chilled cast iron, it could be accurately fitted in order to spin on parallel axle arms, which were grooved to ease oil distribution. Collinge's 'box' used machined left and right hand threaded nuts. An illustration of how good these were is provided by the fact that, whereas it had been necessary to oil the old boxes on axles every 100 miles, Besant's type needed this treatment only every 3,000 miles, and Collinge's every 5,000. Tyres became thinner, until by 1820 mail coaches had tyres only 2½ in. wide (compared with tyres varying in width from 9 in. to 14 in. that had been common two centuries before!). The unladen weight of these coaches was eventually cut down to 16 cwt.

The so-called 'Salisbury Boot', made from a leather covered iron frame mounted rigidly above the front axle-beds, was used by the coachman, who earlier had a seat that was not part of the coach's frame, so that he would be jolted awake. Regulations prevented both mail and stage coaches from carrying as many passengers as they wanted to, although it is doubtful whether they were ever strictly enforced. They can be summarised as follows:

Act	No. on roof	No. of horses
1788	8 (include 2 on driver's box)	
1790	7 (include 1 on driver's box)	3 or more
1806	12 (10 in winter)	4
1811	None, if coach was only 4 ft 6 in. wide	

Shillibeer Omnibus. Pl. 6, 7

It was on 4 July 1829 that George Shillibeer began to run his famous bus service between Paddington Green and the Bank of England. The fare for the entire route was one shilling, and between Islington and either terminus, sixpence. The first series of single-deckers introduced by Shillibeer were pulled by three horses reined side-by-side. The body had seats along the sides that could cater for 22 passengers, and was mounted on four longitudinal full-elliptic springs attached to the 'ex-beds' of a conventional perch undercarriage. The entrance door was situated in the back of the vehicle. The word 'Omnibus', although brought to this country by Shillibeer, had originated with one M. Baudry of Nantes (France), who had an 18-seater omnibus operated by Jacques Lafitte to pick up members of the general public as well as the patrons of his bathing pool. This omnibus ran at stated times of the day. Shillibeer had a special tread plate concealed below the floor of his buses, and this automatically counted the passengers as they entered the saloon. However, it angered certain people so much that in a fracas outside the York-shire Stingo public-house one evening it was smashed up.

The second batch of omnibuses built by Shillibeer were pulled by a pair of horses, since the authorities objected to three animals abreast on the grounds that this was too wide. In consequence a third or even a fourth horse was kept in reserve for attachment when a steep hill had to be negotiated. Another result was that the internal seating capacity was reduced to sixteen, but a further two could be accommodated outside on either side of the driver. So-called 'perchless' springs were fitted to the axles. Inside a check string was positioned centrally along the ceiling of the saloon. The other end of this went through a large wooden ring on the driver's arm. When a passenger wished to alight, he merely pulled the string! This system of stopping the vehicle lasted until the 1870s. By 1834 Shillibeer was part-owner of 60 buses and 600 horses. Because other proprietors copied the word 'Omnibus' on their side panels, Shillibeer retaliated by having his own name substituted as a 'fleet name'.

Greenwood's Three-Horse Bus

John Greenwood began a short stage coach service between Manchester (Market Street) and Pendleton in 1824. His first vehicles were small 12-seater single-deckers, and as in all 19th-century buses the passengers sat in the lower saloon on longitudinal benches facing inwards. They would have been drawn by two horses.

In 1852 Greenwood introduced a much larger and quite novel omnibus. Pulled by three horses abreast, it was a very wide vehicle, and carried a total of 42 passengers, an almost unbelievable number for the middle of the last century. This feat was achieved by carrying seventeen inside, and the remainder seated facing outwards on three sides of the roof. Footrests prevented people from falling too easily from their lofty stations. In addition, no less than two passengers were able to sit on each side of the driver! Brakes were applied to the wheels by operating a treadle, which was located on the driver's footboard. Another in-

novation was a bell placed under the driver's seat, so that the conductor on a monkey board at the rear of the vehicle could communicate with his mate. Although Holtzapffel had tried to introduce a bell pulled by a cord inside the lower saloon in London in 1839, this had not been adopted by the operators. These large vehicles enabled Greenwood to slash the fare for the route (payable at the yard of the Horse Shoe Inn) from 6d. to 3d.

Menzies in Glasgow also operated wide three-horse buses on local routes in the city at this time. His version sat twenty on the lower deck and nineteen on the roof. Some of his buses were tried out in London on the Kingsland Gate to Bank route, but they were probably too wide for regular use in the Metropolis. During the closing decades of the 19th-century, a rush hour route between Highgate and the City, via Islington, was worked by 48-seat double-deckers pulled by three horses and running in the fleet of 'Favorites', originally operated by Messrs. Wilson of Holloway, and taken over by the L.G.O.C. in the 1850s.

Adams' Knifeboard. Pl. 8, 9

By 1845 it was becoming the practice during the incipient London 'rush hours' for some city gentlemen to perch themselves on the curving roofs of the single-decker buses, rather than wait for the next bus or walk to their station. Adams & Company at their Fairfield Works, Bow, built an improved bus with a clerestory roof that gave more headroom inside the saloon. At the same time they provided a centrally placed longitudinal seat along the roof, with a foot-rest preventing top-deck passengers' boots from breaking the glass of the windows of the lower deck, and indeed preventing the passengers from falling into the street below when the bus jolted on the uneven road surface. Access to the roof was by a narrow series of iron tread plates beside the back door of the bus. This vehicle was heavier than the Shillibeers of the second generation. The Adams were commissioned by the Economic Conveyance Company for their London routes.

As a result of the Great Exhibition of 1851 in Hyde Park, many of the Metropolitan operators fitted these longitudinal seats to the roofs of their single-deckers as crowds of tourists flocked into London by rail to visit the Crystal Palace. Eventually a lasting nickname was given to this type of bus when a Leech cartoon showing a bus of this type appeared in *Punch* (15 May 1852) with the caption: 'You don't catch me coming out on the *knifeboard* again to make room for a party of swells.' (My italics.)

These buses were lit by dim oil lamps, which were an open invitation to pickpockets every evening. James Joyce in his *The Story of Passenger Transport in Britain* (1967) (p. 122) aptly describes another aspect of these vehicles. 'There was of course no heating. The best they could do in this direction was a mass of straw on the floor, and this was intended not only as some kind of insulation to keep your feet warm, but also as a general repository for mud and any other variety of dirt that might find its way downwards.'

Miller's Improved Knifeboard.
Pl. 10–12

The newly-formed London General Omnibus Company held a competition for the design of a new double-decker bus in 1856. The winning entry, out of 75 submitted, was that of R. F. Miller of Hammersmith. Miller's bus had a clerestory roof on which was mounted a single longitudinal seat for the offside passengers only. These travellers were protected by a handrail, whilst metal plates replaced the previous rungs for ascending and descending from the top deck. Although Miller had carried off the prize, the L.G.O.C. modified his design

in so far as a knifeboard seating arrangement was adopted, by which five a side could be seated upstairs, together with one passenger on each side of the driver. With twelve seats in the lower saloon this brought in the standard 26-seater of the latter half of the 19th century. Most of the L.G.O.C's earlier buses had their roofs heightened by a foot or eighteen inches, and were converted into modified Millers.

One of the rejected designs was by T. B. Ashford, who produced a so-called 'Saloon Omnibus', in which the passengers on the top deck sat on longitudinal seats facing one another, their feet resting in a curved well in the centre of the roof. Entry to the lower deck was by means of doors on both the nearside and the offside of the back of the vehicle. The Metropolitan Saloon Omnibus Company, which operated between 1857 and 1859, purchased fifteen of these Ashfords.

In April 1881 the newly formed London Road Car Company introduced three unusual knifeboards with a front entrance to the lower saloon, and twin front staircases to the roof. These vehicles had tiny front wheels that were contained within the framework of the chassis. During 1882/3 these buses were rebuilt by the L.R.C.C. on more orthodox lines with a rear entrance, platform and staircase.

From 1860 onwards many of the knifeboards were fitted with so-called 'decency boards' that served both to prevent passengers from falling off the roof and to shield them from the upward gaze of passers-by, which might in particular light on the ankles of the few bold young ladies who dared to climb on to the top deck.

London Road Car 'Garden Seat'
Type. Pl. 13, 16–19

Later, in 1881, the L.R.C.C. began to place in service a revolutionary kind of horse-bus, revolutionary to London that is, since in Europe such buses had been common since the 1850s. In place of the knifeboard seating arrangements, there were so-called 'garden seats', wooden two-seater benches with backs, placed in pairs along the top deck on either side of a central gangway. In place of the metal plate vertical 'stairs', a proper staircase in a curved form was positioned at the rear of the bus. The seating capacity remained at 26, although a few did seat 28. The driver's box was carried on an outrigger, and at first passengers could still sit on either side of him. The L.R.C.C. used deeply cranked axles in order to lower the floor of the saloon, but this did not appear to be very popular, and the L.G.O.C. did not follow suit. Instead they concentrated on enlarging the mounting platform towards the size that we associate with the motorbus. The cost of one of the 1881 vintage L.R.C.C. garden seats was £150, and they were expected to have a life of about twelve years.

By 1895 brakes had begun to be fitted to the wheels of buses to make them safer in the congested traffic conditions in London and other big cities. The previous year an interesting experiment was carried out in Liverpool, where a garden seat bus was fitted with electrical batteries by the Electric Motive Power Company. This ran on experimental journeys.

The last garden seat double-decker to operate in London was run by Tillings between Peckham Rye and Honor Oak in South London, and this only ceased to operate on the evening that the First World War started, 4 August 1914. The L.G.O.C. had withdrawn its last garden seat from route 32 (Moorgate Street – London Bridge) on 25 October 1911. In the country as a whole the last *regular* service was by T. Howe & Company between Newcastle upon Tyne and Gateshead, via the High Level Bridge, and this finished on 13 June 1931.

Station Bus. Pl. 20, 21

During the 1870s in rural areas small operators and hotel proprietors began to run small horse drawn vehicles to meet the main trains at local railway stations. These station buses normally provided inside accommodation for eight or ten people. An entrance right at the back of the vehicle was usual. The windows were glazed. Luggage was carried on the roof of the bus. Two such station buses that have been preserved for posterity are the 10-seater that Hendersons of Glasgow built for Lawson's Kirkintilloch service, and one of 1900 employed by the Kent & East Sussex Railway Company to run between Tenterden Railway Station and Tenterden Town.

This practice was retained in the early days of motorbuses, especially in connection with railway companies such as the G.W.R., N.E.R. and L.N.W.R., whilst a number of hotels bought their own small single-deckers.

Horse Charabanc. Pl. 22–25

In *The Commercial Motor* for 14 September 1911 there is a list of current spellings used for the motorised version of this kind of vehicle. It includes 'charabancs', 'char-à-bancs', 'chars-à-bancs', and 'chars-à-banc'. Apparently the Oxford English Dictionary of that period preferred the rendering 'chars-à-bancs'. However, to the ordinary man in the street who enjoyed outings in them, they were, of course, 'charas'!

This particular horse-drawn vehicle seems to have evolved from the private shooting brake of the 1850s. However, the charabanc differed from the brake (out of which also developed the waggonette) in some important features. Firstly, the bench-type seats were placed in rows with room for four or five persons on each seat, in contrast to the inward facing side benches of the body brake, or the back-to-back seats of the built-up brake. Secondly, the floor of the charabanc sloped upwards from the front, in order that the passengers at the rear of the vehicle might be able to see over the heads of those in the front rows and the large hats of late-Victorian and Edwardian ladies. During the 1880s and 1890s these vehicles, drawn by one, or more usually by two, horses, seated around twenty people. In some places, e.g. Jersey, they lasted up until about the outbreak of the First World War, but in most other holiday areas they were gradually replaced during the early years of the present century by their motorised equivalent.

SECTION II: STEAMERS

Trevithick's 'London' Steam Carriage

On Christmas Eve 1801 a strange sight greeted residents of the Redruth-Camborne area of Cornwall, for puffing and rumbling up Camborne Beacon went Richard Trevithick's trial steamer. On board were the inventor and eight invited passengers. The steam carriage had made its debut in Britain. This remarkable tractor was a four-wheeler.

Trevithick had constructed his 'London' steam carriage at Felton's Works in Leather Lane in London. Its chassis was made of wrought iron, and had two longitudinal central members serving additionally as guide bars for the forked piston rod. A single horizontal cylinder was recessed into the boiler. A large flywheel was keyed to the offside of the crankshaft, which carried spur gears, meshing with the corresponding gear wheels on the unsprung back axle. To compensate partially for the lack of comfort, the diameter of the driving wheels was increased to 10 ft! Between its construction in 1802 and its dismantling in 1804, the 'London' managed to achieve speeds of up to 10 m.p.h. However, the vehicle does not appear to have been used on a regular public service, this event having to wait for a further three decades. A stage-coach type of body was used.

Gordon's Mechanical Legged Coach

Between 1824 and 1830 David Gordon built four steam coaches of a rather novel design. They were fitted with six legs (or 'propellers') as well as wheels! Three 'propellers' were attached to each side of the coach, and flat feet were fitted to their ground end. They were operated by a system of cranks and connecting rods. However ingenious this idea was, it was proved by Gurney, Hancock and others that driving wheels could be much more reliable than mechanical legs, and greater speeds could also be attained.

Hancock's 'Infant'. Pl. 26, 27

In 1830, at his Stratford (Essex) workshops, Walter Hancock built his steam carriage 'Infant'. This four-wheeler was designed to carry ten passengers. It was powered by an oscillating engine which was carried on an outrigger behind the back axle. The boiler was vertical and made up of narrow, parallel water chambers (which Bird describes as very much like a modern domestic radiator). A fireplace was situated beneath the boiler, the fire being fanned by bellows worked by the engine. There was a hopper to feed in coke. Incidentally Hancock discovered in 1832 that the coke supplied by Hove Gas Works was of too low a calorific value to be of much use in his steam carriages. It was also very difficult to obtain supplies of coke in country areas through which his machines passed. The 'Infant' had front wheel steering. Four common coach springs were fitted on the axle for each wheel. The 'Infant' was used primarily on the Stratford to London run, but sometimes it took to the Brighton road instead. Later in the same year it was rebuilt as a 14-seater charabanc, the oscillating engine being replaced by a fixed cylinder vertical engine, which was positioned in an enclosed compartment. The final drive was by chain.

Hancock's next steam coach was the 'Enterprise' (1833). This was to act as a 14-seater bus for a route between Paddington and the City (operated by the London & Paddington Steam Carriage Company). The fare was one shilling and it took on average 68 minutes to complete the return journey, varying in speed between 10 m.p.h. and a reported 16 m.p.h., although some sources claim as much as 20 m.p.h. maximum on occasions. The engine worked on a crank (as the 'Infant's' did after its modifications), and iron chains applied the power to the rear wheels. It began the service on 22 April 1833, but was withdrawn on 3 May that year. D. Redmund rebuilt it after purchasing the machine (he was the operating company's engineer), giving the 'Enterprise' his own patent steering gear and elaborate spring wheels. Later he attempted to build his own version from scratch, meanwhile returning the 'Enterprise' to Hancock at Stratford.

1833 was also the year that witnessed the birth of Hancock's 'Autopsy', which was a small vehicle compared with some of the other Hancock steamers. At first it worked on the Finsbury to Pentonville route, but was later transferred to the Paddington–Moorgate route. This machine is usually regarded as the smaller sister of 'Era'. In its original form 'Era' was an 18-seater, ordered by the London & Brighton Steam Carriage Company, which hoped to use it on their proposed route between London and Greenwich. This plan seems to have fallen through, and so Sir James Anderson had it transported to Dublin, where it worked for eight weeks. It was then returned to Hancock's works, where it was rebodied as a 22-seat charabanc, and was placed on active service between Paddington and City Road (Windsor Place). By this time the name 'Era' had been changed to 'Erin', due to its Irish connections.

The last of Hancock's famous quintet of steamers was 'Automaton', completed in 1836. This was a 22-seater, thus making it the highest capacity vehicle passengerwise of all the Stratford carriages. It was powered by a two-cylinder engine with a bore of 9 in. and a stroke of 12 in. and rated at 24 h.p. at 70 r.p.m., the boiler pressure being 70 p.s.i. The heating surface area was approximately 85 sq. ft, while the grate surface was 6 sq. ft. This was a more efficient engine than Gurney's, in that for every pound of coke burnt ten pounds of evaporated water resulted. Speeds in excess of 20 m.p.h. were claimed for 'Automaton'.

By 1836 the trio 'Erin', 'Autopsy' and 'Automaton' were said to have covered 4,200 miles on p.s.v. duties and to have carried no less than 12,761 passengers.

James Steam Drag
During 1824/5 W. H. James constructed a steam drag, which was powered by two separate small two-cylinder engines. There seem to be no reports of this vehicle being placed into regular service pulling passenger trailers.

Five years later James built a large coach seating 15 and weighing 3 tons. This vehicle had two boilers, which had the high pressure of 250 p.s.i. Then in 1832 he built a coach powered by a four-cylinder engine. The cylinders were paired off so that each pair worked one of the driving wheels independently. By this means James made cornering easier. A three-speed variable gear system was adopted, and there was a properly sprung rear axle. Again there seemed to be no takers.

Gurney's 'Royal Patent'
In 1827 Goldsworthy Gurney built a

steam carriage which could accommodate six passengers inside the actual coach body, plus twelve on cross benches on the roof, with an additional man seated beside the driver, making a total of nineteen. The total weight of this vehicle was 70 cwt, although later Gurney was able to reduce this to 35 cwt. The power unit was a two-cylinder engine with a 9-in. bore and an 18-in. stroke, which worked at pressures from 70 p.s.i. to 100 p.s.i. The piston speed was 200 r.p.m. The boiler was made of welded wrought iron. The steam from the tubes collected in a drum on top of the boiler, from where it passed to two large vertical iron plate tubes (separators) where the steam was separated from the water. The dried steam then proceeded to the superheater, and thence via the throttle valve to the engine. There was an auxiliary hand-operated feed water pump to keep up the level of water in the boiler, in case the steam pump broke down. Coke was used, and this resulted in little smoke being emitted. Approximately 5 lb of water was evaporated for every 1 lb of coke. It was necessary to stoke up only at staging posts, and therefore a tender was not needed. However, for the water supply a 60-gallon tank was fixed in a horizontal position under the coach body. Drive was through connecting rods on to cranks at right angles on the rear axle. Only one driving wheel was fixed rigidly to this axle, but on steep hills or along rough road surfaces both wheels were fixed. These driving wheels were five feet in diameter and were given iron tyres 4 to 5 in. in width. Steering was by means of two small pilot wheels carried on a short axle pivoted at the centre to the end of a long curved pole, the other end of which was fixed to the middle of the steering wheel axle-tree. In his book *Roads and their Traffic, 1750–1850* (1970) (p. 166), John Copeland explains how the steering was done. 'When the driver turned the pilot-wheel axle, using a

handle at the end of a long lever, the pilot wheel went along the desired course, turning the steering-wheel axle about its centre and so causing the coach to follow.' A strong spring returned the pilot wheel to its position at right angles to the curved pole. A steam valve was used for driving the engine to operate the handle for the reversing gear.

In 1828 Gurney built his 'Royal Patent' steam carriage, which weighed 2 tons and carried eighteen passengers. Its engine was situated at the rear of the vehicle. Anthony Bird mentions in his *Roads and Vehicles* (1969) a second carriage produced in that year that weighed $3\frac{1}{2}$ tons and could cope with fourteen passengers. This had a 28 h.p. engine. An additional donkey engine kept the feed water pumps and fire blower going when the vehicle stopped. The exhaust was silenced by passing through a flat feed-tank. No actual brakes were fitted to these vehicles, so in order to stop on hills the reverse gear had to be used to free the driving wheels.

On 21 February 1831 Sir Charles Dance began a service between Cheltenham and Gloucester using Gurney steam drags pulling 16-seat trailers. The engine of the drag was mounted on a perch. There was a cranked driving axle, and as in the other Gurneys, only one wheel was normally driven. Dance's service operated in both directions four times a day and averaged between 9 and 12 m.p.h. over the nine miles between the two towns. Each drag consumed 9s. worth of coke each day, compared with 45s. to keep the necessary eighteen horses to run a comparable horse drawn service. Hence the fares charged were only 50% of those charged on the stage coaches. During 1831 the drags ran a total of 3,644 miles and carried 2,666 passengers. Altogether it is believed that Gurney built six or seven of these drags.

However, June 1831 was a black month for Gurney. Large stones were placed on the Gloucestershire highway, and these broke the crank axles. At Glasgow cavalry barracks during a demonstration one of the Gurneys blew up. It may have been the same demonstrator that took three days to cover the 42 miles between Edinburgh and Glasgow and ended up ignominiously being towed by horses into Clydeside.

Messrs. Maudslay & Field built an improved version of the Gurney steam drag, and ran this experimentally, pulling a single-deck horse bus, between Wellington Street and Greenwich in 1833.

Scott Russell's Steam Carriage

John Scott Russell designed a 26-seat steam coach, which came into service in 1834. These vehicles were built at the Grove House Engine Works in Edinburgh and were powered by a two-cylinder vertical engine with equal bore and stroke of 12 in. There were connecting rods to the crankshafts, one for each cylinder, and thence by 2 to 1 spur gearing to a live axle. This back axle was hung on semi-elliptic springs. The carriages towed two-wheel trailers which carried both the water and the fuel, along with room for a further six passengers.

Half-a-dozen of these vehicles entered service with the Steam Carriage Company of Scotland in 1834, and worked their Glasgow to Paisley service for five months. They took on average 40 minutes to cover the seven miles between the two towns. A crew of three was carried, namely a steersman, a stoker and an engineman. Up to 45 passengers were carried on each journey. However, the boiler of one of these blew up after a wheel had struck a large stone and turned the carriage over on to its side. Three of the others were broken up for scrap, whilst the remaining two vehicles were transported to London, where they ran for demonstrations in Hyde Park. As

nobody was interested in purchasing them, they were taken to Hammersmith for breaking up.

Another report speaks of two Scott Russell coaches working routes from London out to Greenwich, Kew and Windsor during 1833. Whether this pair are additional to the six mentioned above is not at all clear.

Dr. Church's Three-Wheelers

In 1835 a Birmingham man, Dr. W. H. Church, designed a carriage for a projected route between his city and London. His steam vehicle was a three-wheeler of rather elephantine proportions. The front (steering) wheel was encased in an ornate half-sphere, and above this on an equally decorated platform sat four passengers, with the driver mounted in a well in the roof between these paired seats. In all, 22 passengers were seated on the fore platform and inside the two coach compartments to the front and rear of the boiler, whilst a further 22 sat on forward or backward facing seats on the roof of the vehicle. Sprung wheels were fitted that appear in contemporary prints to be quite broad, whilst the boiler consisted of a series of water tubes. Unfortunately the public trials of this monster were not a success, and the local businessmen backing the venture withdrew their financial support.

Two years earlier Dr. Church had placed on the road another three-wheeler, on the side of which was inscribed the words 'London & Birmingham Steam Carriage Company – Church's Patent'. This, too, had a centrally placed boiler, with a very flowery top. Forwards of this was a highly decorated stage coach body, and aft half such a body. It was said to have sat a total of 56 passengers. Although the rear wheels were largely enclosed as in the 1835 model, the front wheel was left exposed in this first version. The wheels were noticeably thinner as well. However, neither of Church's attempts to build a vehicle capable of maintaining a speed of 20 m.p.h. for long distances was to come to fruition.

Carrett's Steam Carriage

The Leeds firm of Carrett, Marshall & Company built a three-wheeler steam carriage weighing 5 tons for the Royal Show in 1861. The diameter of the driving wheels was 4 ft and of the leading wheel 3 ft. This was powered by a twin-cylinder engine and employed a spur-gear drive. There was tiller steering that must have placed a great strain on the wrists of the steersman. Various reports give the seating capacity as either eight or nine. After the 1865 Locomotive Act (the notorious 'Red Flag' act) came into effect, this vehicle was sold to Frederick Hodges, who named it 'Fly-by-Night', due to its attempted nocturnal evasions of the tolls and other restrictions that seemed aimed at driving mechanical coaches off the highways.

In the following year Yarrow & Hilditch built an 11-seater for the 1862 London Exhibition. This had a vertical multi-tubular boiler with bore/stroke of 5 in./9 in. The unusual feature of this vehicle was that the 3-ft rear driving wheels were both contained within the main frame, and both were secured by axles. Its laden weight was 2½ tons.

Thomson's Steam Tractor/Trailer.
Pl. 28

R. W. Thomson of Stonehaven, who had experience as a transport engineer in India, designed 6 h.p. traction engines with a vertical boiler mounted amidships, weighing 5 tons, which were assembled by Messrs. Tennant & Co. at the Bowershall Works, Edinburgh. One of these was sold to A. Ritchie, who ran horse buses, and he had a heavy trailer built for him by Messrs. Drew & Burnet, which ran on a single

axle and carried a total of 65 passengers (21 downstairs, and 44 upstairs under an awning). Named 'New Favorite', it commenced operation on the Edinburgh–Portobello route on 2 June 1870. India-rubber tyres 5 in. × 12 in. were fitted to this vehicle. A detachable flange was bolted on the rim after the tyre had been fitted. In wet weather the tyre stuck firm in the mud, while the wheel revolved!

This was soon joined on the route by Andrew Nairn's 8 h.p. three-wheeler steam bus which was powered by a three-cylinder engine with a Field-type boiler. It weighed 7 tons, ran on hemp tyres, and carried a total of 50 passengers (32 down, 18 up). In 1871 it was replaced by 'Pioneer', a 10-tonner from the same stable, which was hired out to Johnston for his Portobello route, on which it was scheduled to complete a dozen round trips each day. After a fire, it fell into the hands of David Charters, who kept up a half-hour frequency on this same route.

The highest capacity was yet to come, for in 1872 Leonard Todd of Leith produced his 'Edinburgh', a four-wheeler, seating a grand total of 70 (no less than 50 of whom sat under a top-deck awning).

Randolph's Twin-engined Steamer

In 1872 Charles Randolph of Glasgow built a 15-ft long steam carriage of a somewhat unorthodox design. This had a raised driving cab at the front, which even had a driving mirror fitted! A steering wheel, rather than a tiller, was provided, thus giving it a 20th-century appearance at its forward end. Two passengers could sit in the driving cab alongside the steersman, whilst a further six were carried in the main compartment (which was not so high) in the central portion of the vehicle. The rear section contained a vertical boiler connected to engines on both the nearside and offside of the chassis. These engines were both twin-cylindered, and worked one of the rear driving wheels independently, by spur gearing. Randolph's carriage weighed $4\frac{1}{2}$ tons, but could only achieve a speed of 6 m.p.h.

Clarkson Chelmsford Steam Bus.
Pl. 29–32

Of all the names associated with the re-emergence of the steam bus in Edwardian times, the most famous, as far as Britain is concerned, is that of Thomas Clarkson of Chelmsford. As early as 1904 Eastbourne Corporation's No. 3 (later registered AP 369) had been in the form of a Clarkson single-decker. Another early South Coast user was the Torquay and District Motor Omnibus Company Ltd., who purchased five during 1903/4 (two being registered as T 292 and T 466). In 1904 the G.W.R. tried out DA 81 on its Wolverhampton to Bridgnorth route, which commenced on 7 November that year, and in the following year another railway company, the L. & S.W.R., bought Clarksons for use on feeder services between Lyndhurst and Milford in the New Forest, and between Exeter and Chagford on the edge of Dartmoor. In the former case the bus sat eighteen passengers and had a luggage rack on the roof capable of holding 15 cwt of cases etc. The Sussex Motor Road Car Company's distinctive steamer with its wrap-round windscreen, BP 319, was tried out by the Vale of Llangollen Engineering Bus & Garage Company in June 1905. They were so pleased that they bought one of their own (CA 150) for their Llangollen to Bettws-y-Coed route later that year. The London Road Car Company placed in service on 8 October 1904 a 14-seater Clarkson and the L.G.O.C. followed suit two days later.

But it was with the purchase by the London Road Car Company of eight Clarksons of a larger size in 1905 that their fame became certain. Buses like LC 2320 had 25 h.p. engines, the power being provided by two high-pressure horizontal double-acting cylinders of 4 in. bore/stroke. A steam generator of the semi-flash type was positioned under the driver's seat, and this was fired by paraffin, using one of Clarkson's patent burners. The water tank held 40 gallons, and this, of course, necessitated the provision of suitably large storage tanks at convenient points on routes. For instance, for the Worthing to Pulborough route there was one at the White Horse, Storrington. Transmission was by means of side chains. It was only necessary to change down in gear when a hill was steeper than 1 in 10.

In September 1907 there were still only five Clarksons licensed in London, but this number increased during the next few months so that by March 1908 30 were operating. Some of these double-deckers were run by Clarkson's own National Steam Car Company, which staged a parade of its vehicles through the streets of central London on 30 October 1909. The operators built their own 34-seat bodies for vehicles such as F 3603, F 5267 and F 8536.

On the other hand the L.G.O.C. decided to sell its twelve Clarksons in October 1909. These particular buses had Lune Valley boilers, were two-cylinder and were rated at 30 h.p. The final drive was by chain. The chassis were 5 ft 9 in. wide, had a wheel base of 11 ft and stood 2 ft 10 in. off the ground. Their unladen weight was 4 tons 14 cwt. This latter factor made them unacceptable to the Metropolitan Police, who had insisted in the Metropolitan Stage (Motor) Carriages Conditions of September 1909 that no bus should exceed $3\frac{1}{2}$ tons in unladen weight.

In isolated places after this date the Clarkson soldiered on. In 1911 Newton Abbot Motor Omnibus Company proposed to run them on local routes, whilst up in Yorkshire the Harrogate Road Car

Company had built up quite a small fleet of steamers (e.g. C 5919, and T 292, ex-Torquay), beginning in 1906.

The London General had experimented with a light Clarkson 23 h.p. engine being fitted to a De Dion-Bouton chassis with a wheel base of 14 ft and width of 5 ft 10 in., with transmission by means of rack and pinion drive. However, this, too, was up for sale in September 1909, although its unladen weight was of the permitted $3\frac{1}{2}$ tons. Another experiment carried out in London was in November 1913 when a certain Mr. K. S. Broom of Harringay demonstrated how he could be literally swept up off the road surface by one of his patent 'Broom guards' fitted to the front of a Clarkson steamer. The gap between chassis and road surface made some safety device to prevent children and others falling under a bus essential.

Darracq-Serpollet Steamer

Leon Serpollet developed a flash-type generator/boiler in which steam was produced as it was needed. This eliminated the possibility of explosions, while at the same time allowing very high pressures. As Andrew Jamison remarks in his book *The Steam Powered Automobile* (p. 40), 'He also replaced the coke-burning engines that had followed the wood-burning ones with a new engine that used oil, or paraffin, as its fuel.' The bore/stroke of the engine used on the double-deck version were 85 mm/120 mm, which brought about a rating of 30/40 h.p. The burners used a mixture in which the proportion of fuel to water was 1 : 9. There were two double-acting pistons. The rectangular burner with its sixteen nipples, which were for the emission of vaporised paraffin, was positioned where the engine was in a petrol-engined bus. A blow lamp was needed to start the vehicle up when it was cold. The wheelbase was 13 ft 6 in.

The prototype for service in Britain had a body built by the Bristol Carriage and Wagon Company. The Metropolitan Steam Omnibus Company put its first Darracq-Serpollet on to the streets of London on 5 October 1907, and by the summer of 1908 there were twenty of these vehicles licensed. One of them, with a Dodson body, had appeared at the 1908 Olympia exhibition. By September 1911, the Metropolitan, which had for long run on the routes Barnes to Hammersmith, and Barnes to Piccadilly Circus, had 52 newer Darracq-Serpollets, and was planning to increase this number to 100. To cope with a fleet of this size its Chelsea garage was equipped in May 1912 with a new 36,000-gallon tank for storing paraffin, since it was reckoned that each bus consumed 28 gallons of this fuel each day.

In March 1909 the Metropolitan tried out a single-deck version, smartly attired in a green and white livery. This had a 20-seat rear-entrance Dodson body, which had the Leitner electric lighting system, supplied with power by a small dynamo, which in its turn was driven by a leather belt from the second motion shaft of the engine.

In March 1908, a Darracq-Serpollet double-decker was able to cover the hilly road between London and Maidstone (70 miles) in 2 hrs 26 min., when inaugurating a new express route between those two places.

A. H. Creeth & Sons of Nettlestone (Isle of Wight) took delivery of Darracq-Serpollets in 1908, 1909 and 1913. They had 16-seat charabanc bodies.

Gillette Steam Lorry Chassis Bus.
Pl. 33

In January 1899 the Motor Omnibus Syndicate tried out a Gillette steamer in the London area. The chassis was a steam lorry one and on this had been mounted a horse bus body, seating ten passengers inside and fourteen on the top deck, which was covered by an awning with a hole cut in it to allow the chimney to reach towards the heavens. Fore-carriage steering was incorporated in the design. The Gillette never entered regular service, perhaps because it was too clumsy a hybrid, which carried too few fares to make it a viable proposition. It had almost equal-size wheels, had a horizontal boiler (indeed the frontal appearance was rather like that of 'Puffing Billy'), and was driven by side chains on to the rear wheels.

LIFU Steamer

The Liquid Fuel Engineering Company of East Cowes in the Isle of Wight built a range of LIFU steam buses at the end of the 19th century. In 1898 it was, first of all, offering to build and supply a 14-seat waggonette, where the boiler was positioned between the driver's seat and the main body of the vehicle. A 40-gallon oil tank (sufficient for 80 miles) and an 80-gallon water tank (enough for 25 miles) were situated under the chassis. The vehicle's speed on the flat was reckoned to be between 12 and 18 m.p.h.

The single-deck omnibus version had a capacity for 22 seated passengers, two of whom were located next to the driver, a further eight in a compartment with open sides behind this, and the remainder in an enclosed saloon beyond a luggage space. The tanks were as for the smaller waggonette, and the speed was down to an average of 7 to 10 m.p.h. on the level. One of these vehicles with a body built by H. A. House was tried out in London in 1897 with the legend 'Pioneer' across the front of the boiler, which was situated forward of the driver. This bus had wheels shod with strips of rubber, with an iron tyre fitted on top. By the following year this bus had passed into the hands of the Mansfield Motor Car Company, but the company abandoned it after a few months due to constant breakdowns. The Edinburgh Autocar Company placed into service an 18-seater LIFU,

but it was sold with the rest of the fleet when the firm went bankrupt in July 1901. Down in the South East, the Dover & East Kent Motor Bus Company began operations in 1899 with a trio of LIFUs on a route between Dover and Deal, but owing to the high cost of maintenance, this operator also folded up in 1901.

A 28-seat charabanc with luggage space for half a ton on its roof was the third model offered by LIFU. It was only in the way that its body was divided into three equal sections with side doors and curtains for the open sides that this version differed from the bus form.

This manufacturer itself closed down during 1901/2, and eventually the premises became the famous Saunders-Roe aircraft factory.

Thornycroft Steam Bus. Pl. 34

On 17 March 1902 the London Road Car Company placed into service on its route from Oxford Circus to Hammersmith a Thornycroft steamer. Basically, this was a horse bus body fitted onto a steam chassis, with an extended top deck reaching above the driver's seat, and through which the chimney protruded, the whole being topped by an awning carried on side struts. It sat 36 passengers. Steel tyres were fitted to the large rear wheels and the much smaller front wheels. To cope with emergencies a sand box was fitted to the sides of the body-work. Fore-carriage steering was fitted. After a disagreement between the L.R.C.C. and Thornycrofts, the 'Two-penny Lodging House', as it was rudely called, was exported to Port Elizabeth in South Africa.

A year before this the Italian pioneer of radio, Gugliemo Marconi, had employed a single-decker bus version of the Thornycroft steamer for some experiments based on the Haven Hotel, Poole (Dorset). It was from here that Marconi was transmitting messages to and from the Needles Hotel across the Solent in the

Isle of Wight. The bus was fitted with a long cylindrical aerial to the roof of its rear-entrance saloon body, and then driven to a fixed spot, where it became a receiving station. At this stage it was not possible to pick up messages by radio whilst the vehicle was in motion.

SECTION III: ELECTRIC

Bradford Trolleybus. Pl. 35

Between 1913 and 1920 Bradford Corporation decided to construct its own vehicles for the extension of its trolleybus system. In all, the Corporation built eighteen single-deckers and a pair of double-deckers, but the latter come outside the period of this volume. The single-deckers were numbered 503–20, and later received the registrations AK 9621–37/9 (but not in a corresponding sequence).

These Bradford trolleybuses were powered by two 20 h.p. Siemens motors, as had been their predecessors, the four R.E.Ts. These motors enabled a maximum speed of 23 m.p.h. to be achieved on the level, and drove twin-worm and worm wheels, in place of the side chains of the earlier trolleybuses working in the city. The overall length of the 29-seater vehicle was 23 ft 2 in., of which the portion containing the rear entrance saloon measured 15 ft. The Bradford-built trolleybuses weighed half a hundredweight short of 4 tons.

These vehicles are quoted as consuming 1·2 units per car mile. This compares with 1·5 units per car mile for the double-decker No. 521 (later AK 9638), which at 7 tons 8¾ cwt was a much larger vehicle than these single-deckers. Indeed, with its 51 seats and its height of 15 ft 4 in., it must have seemed a vast vehicle to the Bradfordians of 1920. It was powered by a single Dick Kerr 45 h.p. motor, such as was used in tramcars. The final drive was by gear and chain.

Its maximum speed on the level was 18 m.p.h.

Brush-Cleveland Trolleybus.
Pl. 36, 37

On 10 March 1913 Stockport Corporation commenced trolleybus operations on a route between the Town Centre and Offerton, using three Brush-bodied and -chassised trolleybuses numbered 1–3. They were powered by Cedes-Stoll motors and sat 28 passengers, having an open platform at the rear. The method of current collection in this instance was by the Bremen, or Lloyd-Kohler, system. In this method the two wires were placed one above the other, the negative being in the top position. A loose cable connected the trolley wheel to the vehicle. When two vehicles met they had to exchange trolleys. The service finished on 7 October 1919, and subsequently one of the Stockport vehicles was sold to Mexborough & Swinton Traction Company, which numbered it as 24 in its fleet, and replaced the Lloyd-Kohler equipment with orthodox British trolley booms.

On 22 December 1914 the Rhondda Tramways Company began a service of single-decker trolleybuses between Williamstown and Gilfach Goch. Unfortunately due to subsidence the road became impassable at Llantrisant the following month, and owing to wartime shortages it was not possible for the local council to find the necessary materials to effect the repair. The chassis were built by the Cleveland Car Company of Darlington with Brush bodywork. They were probably numbered 53–58. Shortly after the Tees-side trolleybus system started, the Rhondda vehicles were sold to this new operator, and became Nos. 11–16 (AJ 5866–71) in its fleet.

Since R.E.T. failed to complete an order for ten trolleybuses to inaugurate the North Ormesby-Grangetown/Normanby routes in 1919, the newly formed Tees-side Railless Traction Board placed its order with Cleveland, who supplied the chassis, on which were fitted English Electric bodies. Dick Kerr supplied the motors, and Nos. 1–10 (AJ 5857–65) began working on Saturday 8 November 1919.

Cedes-Stoll Trolleybus. Pl. 38, 39

The first trial of a Cedes-Stoll trolleybus in Britain seems to have been that in Greengate Street, West Ham, in September 1912 during the holding of the Municipal Tramways Association Conference there. The first system to adopt the Cedes-Stoll method was Keighley Corporation in Yorkshire which began working on 2 May 1913, on the Ingrow to Lees route. Its first trolleybus (No. 0 !) had a pair of 20 h.p. Cedes motors, and when built (in 1913) had an imported Austrian 24-seat front-entrance single-deck body. Next year followed Nos 1 & 2 with Dodson 28-seat rear entrance body and powered by pairs of Johnson & Phillips 20 h.p. motors. Nos. 3–8 arrived during 1914/15, and differed only in having more powerful motors (twin 25 h.p. in the case of 3/4, and twin 28 h.p. in the case of the rest), and one extra seat capacity.

The Cedes-Stoll system at Aberdare U.D.C. in South Wales was inaugurated on 15 January 1914. Here at least five (Nos. 21–25) entered service on a series of four routes (Trecynon Cemetery-Cwmdare; Aberdare-Aberdant; Aberaman-Cwmaman; Aberaman-Capcoch), linked only by the main Trecynon-Aberdare-Aberaman tram route. Indeed the trolleybuses had to be towed by tramcars out from the depot at Gadlys each day to commence operations on their particular route, although they were fitted with a slipper to lower into the tram track so that they could work under their own power along the tram route. These trolleybuses were 20 ft 9 in. long, with a wheelbase of 12 ft 8 in., and were 7 ft 3 in. wide. Their bodies sat 27 passengers,

were rear-entranced, and were constructed by Christopher Dodson. They were powered by a pair of Cedes motors, which were assembled at the works of Johnson & Phillips at Charlton (London). Writing in *Buses Illustrated* (No. 130, October 1966), A. G. Newman describes the unusual method of current collection thus: 'A four-wheeled trolley ... ran on top of the overhead wires, while the motors were an integral part of the rear wheels. The trolley was connected to the vehicle by a flexible cable wound on to a drum under the bonnet. A plumb-bod hanging from the trolley adjusted the tension on the cable at the upper end. The trolleys were not regarded as being a part of any one vehicle and were freely exchanged in the manner of the London tram plough collectors. Most of the routes in Aberdare were equipped with only one pair of wires, and the trolleys were exchanged as vehicles met. . . . The wires were suspended by J hangers. . . . Hoisting the trolley on to the wires was a difficult operation requiring it to be raised on a forked pole from the top of the vehicle and pushed between the wires. It was then turned through 90° and gently lowered on to the wires.'

On 16 September 1914 Hove Corporation began tests with a 32-seat double-decked Cedes-Stoll painted cream and blue, on a short trial route between Hove Station and Church Road via Goldstone Villas and George Street. When the Cedes-Stoll company in Britain (based on Stamford Hill) was wound up on Government orders in 1916 as being an alien and enemy concern, this double-decker (powered by two 20 h.p. Johnson & Phillips motors) was sold to Keighley Corporation along with much of the overhead. It became No. 9 in that fleet in 1917. Its unladen weight was under 4 tons, giving a laden weight of 5½ tons.

Crompton Battery Bus

In November 1911 the prototype of a new

attempt to capture the omnibus market with a battery-operated vehicle came out of the factory, when F 4857 left the Crompton works with its orthodox double-decked body. Yet once you lifted that bonnet you began to realise that this was no orthodox bus. For under the bonnet lay the batteries, placed there so that they could be easily lifted out by a crane. Transmission in F 4857 was by means of two motors and chain drive to a pair of worm gears acting on the rear wheels: in other words a cross between what Dennis did and what most of the remaining manufacturers continued to do. The motor generator was located between the batteries and the motors. Road trials around Chelmsford suggested that the Crompton had a uniform acceleration rate and a similar pattern for retardation. The battery model was apparently not wanted by the London operators (an earlier Crompton battery bus had been examined by the L.G.O.C. in 1909). Perhaps they had seen the snags involved with the running of the Electro-buses. At the same time there were not yet enough municipalities operating motorbus services to attract clients. The same happened a few years later in the case of the Edison battery vehicle.

Daimler Trolleybus. Pl. 40

The only system to buy trolleybus chassis from Daimlers during our period was the first company (as opposed to municipality) to run trolleybuses in Britain: the Mexborough & Swinton Traction. On 31 August 1915 trolleybuses commenced running on routes to Manvers Main and Conisbrough, using a fleet of three vehicles, numbered 21–3, which sported 28-seat single-decker Brush bodies with rear entrances. However, on 16 April 1917 these services had to be withdrawn due to staff shortages. The Manvers Main route was reopened in 1919, but the other route did not restart until 1922.

Edison Battery. Pl. 41–43

In 1915 West Bromwich Corporation bought four Edison chassis powered by electric batteries, and had the W. J. Smith bodies transferred from their Albion A12s and also their registrations (EA 300–3). In December of the next year Lancaster Corporation followed suit with a pair of Edisons (Nos. 1, B 5981 and 2, B 5979), fitted with Brush 22-seat front-entrance bodies. A third Brush-bodied vehicle (No. 3, B 5982) followed in January 1917. In 1918 a fourth and fifth Edison were added to this north-western municipal fleet with the arrival of No. 4 (B 5998) and No. 5 (B 5934). These two had rather weird looking 22-seat bodies built by the local coachbuilding firm of Hardy. In 1917 Oldham Corporation contemplated re-placing the 'unsatisfactory Coal Gas driven Bus on the Coppice Section by one Electrically driven' (Tramways Committee minutes for December 13th), following their successful operation of an electric battery tower waggon. However, in February 1918 it was learnt that the Ministry of Munitions had refused permission for the purchase of an electric chassis, and so Oldham never joined the select 'club' of battery operated bus fleets. Southend-on-Sea Corporation was actually the first to place an Edison in service, way back in 1914. HJ 34 had a rather ignominious end two years later when it had its bus body removed and was converted into a coal lorry for the use of the borough Electricity Engineer's Department. Derby Corporation bought one (No. 2, CH 1812) in 1919, and South Shields Corporation tried one out in 1914.

The chassis was propelled by an electric motor supplied by A8-type 300 amp./hrs capacity batteries, which took five hours to recharge every night. In Lancaster a booster plant was provided in the Market Square to enable the batteries to recharge partially before the buses proceeded on their way to either Skerton or Marsh. They were also employed to convey workers to the munitions factory in Caton Road. They were used as pay-as-you-enter buses.

Electrobus. Pl. 44

The London Electrobus Company appeared on the scene in 1906 with its own interesting vehicles, which proved to be the only battery-operated double-deckers to have any successful period of service in Britain. They were powered by 14 h.p. French Thompson-Houston electric motors, which were connected with 44-cell batteries, weighing 23 cwt, and slung under the chassis. The Electrobus was 6 ft 3 in. wide. When in the Autumn of 1908 one of these vehicles was fitted with an experimental unglazed canopy over the top deck, and this idea was turned down by the Metropolitan Police, the Editor of *The Commercial Motor* commented that he felt the heavy weight of the batteries carried by each Electrobus was quite sufficient to make them stable enough for roofing to be provided: after all, trams in London had roofs! There was a live axle driven by a bevel wheel at the end of the prop shaft. Because of the ample supply of electricity from their batteries, the Electrobuses were brilliantly lit inside, and as from November 1907 a standard light was also fixed to the nearside rear corner of the top deck. In this case three incandescent lamps were fixed to white saucer-shaped reflectors, which enabled every top deck passenger to read his newspaper easily on the way home in the dark! A further plan to display illuminated advertisements on the 'tween decks panels was thwarted by Scotland Yard in February 1909.

LC 5768, the prototype, entered service on 15 July 1907, and gradually the fleet run by the London Electrobus Company reached double figures, the fourteenth bus becoming operational in June 1908. By that time these battery vehicles were working two central routes, namely: Earl's Court to Liverpool Street, and Brondesbury to the Law Courts. The fleet reached its maximum strength of twenty by the end of the year.

However, as early as October 1908 the firm began negotiations with Brighton Corporation, Hove Corporation and Torquay Corporation for selling some of its buses. But it was not until the withdrawal of the fleet on 31 March 1910 that many of these vehicles travelled to the South Coast for the remainder of their natural lives. Already in the previous year the Brighton, Hove & Preston United Omnibus Company had purchased three Electrobuses (CD 775, 806/7), and now that operator bought the twelve buses still stationed in London. Eight entered service, whilst the remainder were dismantled for spares, their bodies passing on to new Hallford-Stevens petrol-electrics as CD 874/80/7. The Electrobuses were finally retired in 1916.

Radcliffe Ward Battery Bus

In January 1889 the Ward Electrical Car Company secured police permission to operate an electric battery bus on trials, in the hope of starting a regular public service in July of that year. It could travel at 7 m.p.h., and the *Financial Times* of 11 February 1889 described its appearance as resembling 'a large and rather cumbrous omnibus'.

Two years later Bersey started a demonstration service using perhaps the same vehicle. It ran between Charing Cross and Victoria, carrying a load of 26 passengers, 14 of whom sat on the top deck. Due to the weight of 72 Sola accumulators that gave it power, it topped the $3\frac{1}{2}$ ton mark unladen. Like other early battery buses, it only achieved low speeds, and so it was soon withdrawn from active service.

Railless Electric Traction. Pl. 45–50

In the closing days of September 1909

the Metropolitan Electric Tramways Company tried out a Railless Electric Traction single-decker trolleybus on a 'U' shaped wiring system with a turning loop at both ends. The vehicle concerned was powered by two 25 h.p. electric motors manufactured by B.T.H. on a chassis built by James & Browne Ltd. of Hammersmith. Each motor weighed almost 18 cwt and drove one of the rear wheels through a bevel gear and Renold silent chains. The overall weight of the vehicle was in excess of 6 tons. The trolley pole and other electrical fittings were produced by Messrs. Brecknell, Munro & Rogers of Bristol, whilst Milnes & Voss built the 24-seat rear-entrance body, which was numbered as trolleybus No. 1 in the M.E.T. fleet, and bore on its sides the mythical legend 'The Burroughs-Hendon-Golder's Green Station'. The issue of *Electrical Industries & Investments* dealing with this experiment within the confines of the M.E.T. Hendon depot describes the vehicle as 'somewhat peculiar. It looks like a single-deck petrol omnibus, but the trolley arm on the roof introduces an unfamiliar note.' However, although the Editor thought that such a trolleybus route feeding to the tube at Golder's Green or the trams at Finchley would be a boon, it was not to be, for by the time the scheme to implement it had got to the planning stage (in 1911) the L.G.O.C. had extended its motorbus route as far as Child's Hill, and brought the new and highly successful 'B' class double-deckers into the Hendon area.

Thus it was not until 20 June 1911 that Britain's first two permanent trolleybus systems came into operation. One was in Leeds, where the Corporation had installed a route from the City Square to New Farnley at a cost of £1,246 per mile. R.E.T. provided four cars for this route (Nos. 501–4. The first three were later registered as U 8403–5), powered by twin 20 h.p. motors and with Hurst

Nelson 28-seat rear-entrance bodies, which were 15 ft long, mounted on chassis 20 ft 3 in. in length and with a wheelbase of 13 ft. The 525-volt motors operated at 1,050 r.p.m., and were connected with controllers that had nine positions: five series and four parallel. The final drive was by side chains.

A few miles away, Bradford began operations on the same day with another pair of Railless trolleybuses, on a 'network' that had cost £1,654 per mile to build. Like the Leeds trolleys, these R.E.Ts cost £700 apiece. The first route ran from Dudley Hill to Laisterdyke, and was worked by cars 240/1, which also had Hurst Nelson 28-seat rear-entrance bodies. The motors were provided by Siemens. Two years later Nos. 240/1 were replaced by two new Railless vehicles (Nos. 501/2, later registered as AK 4516 and AK 8090). Again twin 20 h.p. Siemens motors of 525 volts and of speed 1,050 r.p.m. were fitted.

Between 5 September 1912 and 13 May 1914 Dundee Corporation ran two R.E.Ts on a route from Maryfield to Fairmuir. Nos. 67/8 were powered by pairs of 20 h.p. Siemens motors and had 28-seat rear-entrance Milnes-Voss bodies, which had open platforms. They were nicknamed 'The Stouries' due to the amount of dust they created in their travels. In 1917 they were sold to Halifax Corporation, and subsequently became Nos. 103/4 (CP 2021/2) in that fleet.

During December 1913 and January 1914 Brighton Corporation tried out a double-decked R.E.T. along London Road from St. Peter's Church to Rose Hill Terrace, with later 'excursions' as far afield as Beaconsfield Villas. This vehicle came from Leeds (the home of Railless), and had a 34-seat body built by them. It was powered by a pair of Johnson & Phillips 20 h.p. motors, which drove the chains attached to the rear wheels. The unladen weight of this bus was $4\frac{1}{4}$ tons. During the trials it bore the fleet number 50.

Prior to these tests, on 3 October 1912, Rotherham had opened its first trolley-bus route between Heningthorpe Lane and Maltby with a trio of R.E.Ts, which were at various times numbered 38–40 and T 1–3. In the following year, on 14 August, Ramsbottom U.D.C. began a route from Holcombe Brook Station to Edenfield with three R.E.T. single-deckers with Milnes-Voss 28-seat front-entrance bodies, which were later replaced by Leeds-built bodies of the same layout constructed by Lockwood & Clarksons. Nos. 1–3 employed the Schie-mann system of current collection.

The final batch of Railless trolleybuses delivered before 1919 went to Leeds in 1915, when Nos. 505–9 (later registered as U 8406–10) arrived, having the same features as the 1911 cars.

SECTION IV: PETROL/PETROL-ELECTRIC 1898–1909

Albion Waggonette

The Albion A3 model appeared on the scene in 1905 powered by a *two*-cylinder 16 h.p. engine. Being in essence a motor-ised version of the horse drawn waggon-ette that had plied for hire in the rural areas for the later decades of the Victor-ian era, the A3 found its clientele in similar surroundings, especially in its native Scotland. For instance the Suther-land Motor Traffic Company of Golspie bought an 11-seater (NS 21) in that first year, as did the Kingstown & Bray Motor Service. Gareloch Motor Service of Helensburgh purchased a pair for its route between Helensburgh, Clynder and the Head of Gareloch. One of these (SN 185) is quoted as a 7-seater charabanc! The Sutherland operator came back for three more with charabanc bodies in 1906 (NS 10, NS 17 and NS 42), while in 1907 Glasgow Parish Council bought

one fitted with a 14-seat front-entrance bus body (G 1230) for the use of people seeking parochial relief!

A four-cylinder version of this small Albion chassis took the fancy of Wolver-hampton Corporation in 1911, when it was thinking of taking into stock some motorbuses. No. 1 (DA 684) and its sister of 1912 vintage (No. 2, DA 306) were given Forder 24-seat charabanc bodies. Nearby the proprietor of the Cross Hotel, Kingswinford purchased a pair of these 30 cwt chassis in 1911, and had W. J. Smith of West Bromwich fit 18-seat bus bodies to them.

Armstrong-Whitworth 32 h.p.

From the Scotswood (Newcastle upon Tyne) factory of Armstrong, Whitworth & Company at the beginning of 1907 came a 32 h.p. chassis with a four-cylinder engine of $4\frac{5}{16}$ in. bore and $5\frac{1}{2}$ in. stroke, which gave 32 h.p. at 900 r.p.m. There was a leather-covered cone clutch and a four-speed gearbox. The final drive was by side chains. The prototype (LN 371) had a double-deck body of the usual rear-entrance open-top design, that had become standard by the mid-Edwardian epoch. The only London operator that seems to have purchased any of this make was the L.M.O.C. In September 1907 it had only one Arm-strong-Whitworth in service, but by November 1908 it had increased this to ten. There was an Armstrong-Whitworth chassis on display at the 1908 Olympia Show.

Arrol Johnston 24 b.h.p. Pl. 52

The Paisley firm of Arrol Johnston was a well-known manufacturer of p.s.v. chassis during the first decade of this century. In 1905 it was offering a four-cylinder vehicle that was said to develop 24 b.h.p. at 950 r.p.m. The bore was $4\frac{1}{4}$ in. and the stroke 5 in. This model had a Hele-Shaw metal-to-metal friction disc clutch, and an enclosed differential shaft and roller chains. Because many of its customers operated in areas where the roads were very rough (e.g. the North British Railway Company bought from Arrol Johnston XS 68, a 14-seat charabanc), a three point suspension was incorporated, and this was designed to counteract the twisting of the main frame on such routes. The first Arrol Johnston p.s.v. was in fact XS 38, which went to Fylde Motor Services, Bispham, in 1904.

Although the first Arrol Johnston in London service began work on 24 November 1906 for the London & District Motor Bus Company (the 'Arrow' fleet), by September 1907 there were only five Arrol Johnstons in service in London, but with the advent of a new model in 1908 this number quickly increased to 30, most of which entered service with G.E.R. These buses had larger radiators than any other contemporary London bus, and *The Commercial Motor* noted that their fuel consumption was 6·2 m.p.g., which was deemed 'worthy of special mention'. The Hele-Shaw clutch was retained, but the 30-gallon petrol tank had been removed from under the driver's seat, and was now positioned at the rear of the chassis. The final drive was by means of a prop shaft and spring drive.

By 1909 the manufacturers were offering a small 12–15 h.p. p.s.v. chassis, and Messrs. Brown and Findlay of Dundee purchased one of these for their Lochee to Muirhead route, and had it fitted with an 18-seat body.

Beaufort 30/35 h.p.

This model first appeared in 1906, when it was powered by a four-cylinder engine of bore/stroke of 120 mm/130 mm, and was stated to develop 30 h.p. at 750 r.p.m. By the Olympia Show of the following year it was rated at 35 b.h.p. at 1,000 r.p.m. The Beaufort had a leather-faced cone clutch, which was connected to a hollow cardan shaft. There was a

four-speed gearbox of the sliding type. The final drive was by means of roller chains, and in 1907 customers were offered a choice of having either Morse or Renold silent chains fitted. There were also two ignition systems – high tension by coil and accumulator, and low tension magneto. The wheelbase was 13 ft 3 in. The L.G.O.C. was the only metropolitan operator interested in the Beaufort, and gave a trial to the 1906 version (e.g. LC 8512) with double-deck body fitted in 1907.

Beaufort also offered a 24 h.p. chassis suitable for charabanc work.

Brush-Mutel 25 h.p. Pl. 54

We usually associate the Loughborough firm of Brush with bodywork, but in Edwardian times it was trying to establish itself as a manufacturer of chassis as well. In 1905 the Potteries Electric Traction Company took delivery of three chassis powered by 25 h.p. Mutel engines, but with Brush bodywork. EH 1 and EH 2 had small 18-seat *double-deck* bodies with a *front* staircase that partially obscured the driver's nearside view. EH 4, on the other hand, had a 23-seat charabanc body.

There followed the Brush 'B' type with a 40 h.p. engine. Another member of B.E.T., the Birmingham & Midland Motor Omnibus Company, bought nine of this model in 1906, and had them given 36-seat Milnes double-decker bodies (O 1283–91). These were later dispersed in 1908 among other B.E.T. companies, viz. O 1283–6/8/91 went down to Kent for Deal & District Motor Services, O 1286 having a front-entrance single-deck body on it by that time. O 1287/9/90 were hired out to the Leamington & Warwick Electric Company. The Brush 'B' was in advance of its time in that it incorporated Dennis worm drive, in place of the almost universal side chains.

The London-based Amalgamated

Motor Bus Company operated some Brush 'C' type double-deckers in 1906 (e.g. LC 6309 & LN 9788), but the Brush was never a 'hit' with the capital's operators. LN 9788, now with a 33-seat charabanc body, ended up in the ranks of the Worcester Electric Traction Company, as did Brush 'B' registered U 771.

At the 1907 Olympia Show, Brush exhibited a 35 h.p. model with the rather large bore/stroke measurements 5 in./6 in. There was an internal cone clutch, and a large differential was fitted to the live rear axle.

Cannstatt-Daimler Double-decker.
Pl. 66

At the end of April 1898 the Hon. C. S. Rolls imported a single-decker 12 h.p. Cannstatt-Daimler from Germany. On 3 October 1902 a second chassis built by Cannstatt and powered by a Daimler engine, and with an unwieldy body constructed to a design by Harry John Lawson, entered service between Lewisham and Eltham. It sat twelve passengers inside and a further fifteen outside, including one seated next to the driver, high up above the bonnet. It was withdrawn early in 1904. It was the first *large* bus to be fitted with solid rubber tyres.

Earlier, on 9 October 1899, the Motor Traction Company started a service between Kennington and Victoria Station, crossing the Thames by Westminster Bridge, using a pair of German Cannstatt-Daimlers with 26-seat double-decker bodies built by Brazil, Holborough & Straker of Bristol. The bonnet looked rather like that of the future 'Bullnose' Morris Oxford. The vehicles were shod with steel tyres, and were powered by four-cylinder 12 h.p. engines. They were withdrawn from active service in December 1900.

Charron 20/30 h.p. Pullmans
In May 1908 the London Motor Garage

Company supplied the General Motor Cab Company with some de-luxe single-deck Charrons, built in France with 110 mm bore/130 mm stroke engines, the transmission being by the then usual method of side chains. Not such a normal feature, however, was the fitting of Michelin (or in some cases Gaulois) pneumatic tyres to give a more comfortable ride. Other refinements for the nine passengers that each of these rear entrance single-deck Pullman vehicles carried included lighting by electricity and heating. The first of these luxury vehicles (LN 9772) entered service on a central route between Queen's Hall (Portland Place) and Cromwell Road (South Kensington). As on the 'Red Arrow' buses of 60 years later, there was a flat fare of 6d. Editorial comment in *The Commercial Motor* of 14 May stated that 'The passenger catered for by this first service is the Kensington and Mayfair resident, who requires something more than the utilitarian penny-stage motorbus. The vehicles are, and doubtless will be, maintained in a specklessly clean condition, and this feature in itself will tempt the better-clothed members of the community to an extravagance amounting to about two-pence per mile.'

By the end of that month a second route had been started, between Victoria and Piccadilly. But by February 1909 the three Charrons operating on the Queen's Hall to Kensington route had to be withdrawn owing to lack of custom.

By July 1910 a 12-seater Charron Pullman was running between Park Langley Estate (Beckenham) and Beckenham Junction Railway Station. It was equipped with K.T. tyres. One luxury for those days was that a printed timetable was provided for the convenience of the clientele.

Another Pullman was purchased by the famous comedian Fred Karno in the same year, along with a Leyland bus, to transport his No. 1 Company from theatre to theatre.

Commercial Cars 36 h.p. Pl. 55, 89–91
A four-cylinder model with a bore/stroke of 4⅛ in./5⅝ in. and developing 36 b.h.p. at 1,000 r.p.m. appeared at the 1907 Olympia Show. This was available with either an accumulator or a magneto ignition system. There was a four-speed gearbox. The wheelbase was 13 ft. In October that year the dimensions of the bore and stroke are quoted as having been 4½ in. and 5½ in. respectively. A 28-seat charabanc demonstrator running under the trade plate BM 13 B ran between the railway station and the Royal Agricultural Show at Lincoln on Midsummer Day, 1907. The bodywork had a glass window at the rear of the vehicle and curtains were hung along both the open sides. It was later registered as FE 350. Another 36 h.p. was purchased by Stafford Motor Services. E 676 was given a 31-seat rear-entrance bus body by Bayleys, and the measurements of this are quoted as being 23 ft 6 in. long by 7 ft 6 in. wide by 10 ft high.

The next move in the development of the Commer p.s.v. was the design in the closing months of 1907 of what was described as a four-way combination-type of body, viz:

(a) lorry body, with flat tailboard
(b) tilt van body
(c) open waggonette, with spring longitudinal seats
(d) enclosed single-decker omnibus with roof rack.

An offer of a first prize of one guinea for a suitable name for this vehicle was won by *Mrs.* S. West of Catford, who thought up the title 'Convertible'. And as the Commer 'Convertible' it appeared at the 1908 Olympia Show.

Under the designation 'CC' several municipalities took an interest during 1909. For example, Keighley Corporation began to build up their fleet with some of these 36 h.p. chassis. C 3351 and C 3387 bore Chapman 34-seat charabanc bodywork, whilst in the following year C 3685 and C 3686/7 arrived with Stagg & Robson 18-seat single-deck bus bodywork. The more powerful 45 h.p. version was ideal for double-deckers, and Keighley introduced three with 50 seats into their fleet (C 3815 and C 3912/3), all with Stagg & Robson bodies. Across the other side of England, Widnes Corporation made the news with four (B 2163–6) that were given 34-seat Dodson bodies which had permanent roofs, the first in Britain to operate on public service regularly. Widnes opened up a route between the famous Transporter Bridge and Rainhill in 1909. Bolton Corporation also bought Commers at this time. Amongst other operators buying the Luton products in 1909 were the Lancashire & Yorkshire Railway Company (double-deckers), and Provincial, for its Grimsby fleet. No. 5 (EE 705) was a rear-entrance double-decker, while No. 6 (EE 706) had a rear-entrance bus body with an open rear platform, which replaced its original charabanc body. The platform was later enclosed and the vehicle converted to run on gas, a cylinder of which was attached to the rear of the bus. In the Isle of Man J. P. Smith of the Hotel Metropole (Douglas) introduced one of these Commers as the island's first station omnibus, whilst R. S. Dymond & Sons purchased one with a double-deck body for their service between Bideford and Westward Ho. In the East Midlands, Commercial Car Hirers used a 20-seater rear-entrance bus (CH 405) to inaugurate its Ashbourne to Derby route.

In August 1909 Commer introduced a new smaller vehicle weighing 25/30 cwt, and powered by a four-cylinder 90 mm/120 mm engine developing 16 b.h.p. It was claimed that one great merit of this model was that the engine, flywheel, carburettor, starting handle, fan, radiator and clutch were all assembled as one unit for easy replacement. Aluminium chain guards were provided. It was probably this model that attracted the attention of the Midland Great Western Railway in Ireland who took delivery of three in 1910 (IM 179–81) equipped with 15-seat charabanc bodywork. Another has miraculously been preserved for posterity. EC 634 received an 11-seat bus body and was bought by Lord Lonsdale.

Critchley-Norris 40 h.p.

Manufactured at Bamber Bridge, near Preston, the Critchley-Norris 40 h.p. made its debut in 1906 at the Royal Agricultural Hall Show. Its four-cylinder engine had a bore of $4\frac{1}{4}$ in. and a stroke of $5\frac{1}{8}$ in., and this developed 25 b.h.p. at 800 r.p.m. There was an alternative four-cylinder power unit with a bore of $4\frac{3}{4}$ in. and a 6 in. stroke, and this was rated at 30 b.h.p. at 800 r.p.m., increasing to 42 b.h.p. at 1,000 r.p.m. One of the features of this model was a newly designed radiator consisting of 55 tubes set at 10° to the horizontal at each end of the central chamber. These tubes were sealed at both ends and contained a spirit normally below atmospheric pressure. Heat made this vaporise, rise, condense, fall and cool the water. There was a four-speed gearbox and a cone clutch. Transmission was by side chains to sprockets bolted to the rear wheels. The more powerful of the two versions was also displayed at the 1907 Olympia Show. Todmorden Corporation bought two of these buses in 1907. C 1503 was given a rear-entrance single-deck body, whilst its sister C 1504 received a 35-seat double-deck body. Later, in the autumn of that year, their Critchley-Norris engines were replaced by Belsize units.

In 1908 at Olympia, Critchley-Norris exhibited a steam bus chassis. This three-cylinder machine ran at 500 r.p.m.,

accelerating to 800 r.p.m., when it was developing 35 b.h.p. Power was transmitted through two short cardan shafts to a differential countershaft, and from there by side chains to the rear wheels. The steam generator was placed behind the bonneted steam engine, and was a compromise between water tubes and flash types. There was a central cylindrical vessel, round which were external coils of mild steel tubes. The steam reached 500°F. The Rossendale Division Carriage Company, which had purchased a double-deck Critchley-Norris 40 h.p. petrol-engined bus in 1906, had promised to take delivery of this prototype steam bus. In competition with Clarksons and Darracq-Serpollet, this northern challenge seems to have failed, and thereafter this firm quietly disappears from the p.s.v. scene.

Daimler Waggonette. Pl. 56

Small four-wheel waggonettes pulled by a single horse became popular for short excursions during the last two decades of the nineteenth century. One passenger could sit beside the driver, while six others sat facing each other on bench seats above the comparatively large rear wheels. Sometimes these seats were folding or completely removable, so that the vehicle could be used for luggage. From this vehicle developed the station waggon of the twentieth century.

In 1898 the Edinburgh Autocar Company began, on 19 May, what was perhaps the first regular and licensed urban motorbus service in Britain. Between that date and the company's failure three years later Daimler waggonettes were used. London witnessed its first proper service using these imported German machines on 1 April 1901, when the South Western Motor Car Company, an enterprise of Walter Flexman French, opened up a route between Streatham and Clapham Junction. His two waggonettes had 10-seat bodies, two passengers sitting beside the driver. On 18 September 1901 F. J. Bell, who had been working in Bournemouth in 1900, started a more ambitious scheme in London using seven waggonettes on a route between Putney and Piccadilly Circus. His particular vehicles had MMC chassis with solid rubber tyres, and the bodies sat eight, with two seated alongside the driver. These waggonettes were powered by 10 h.p. Panhard-Daimler engines. T. H. Barton claimed to be the first operator of regular motor excursions from a seaside resort in the summer of 1903, when he used a 6 h.p. Daimler waggonette seating twelve passengers for trips from Weston-super-Mare to Wells, Glastonbury and Cheddar Gorge. Earlier he had inaugurated a route between the Old Pier and the New Pier at Weston with this vehicle.

Five Daimler waggonettes were built for the Plymouth Motor Car Company in 1900.

One Daimler waggonette that started running between Whitstable and Herne Bay in Kent in 1900 was still working this route ten years later, in spite of the fact that it was competing with the railway between these two towns, and also charging higher fares than its rivals!

De Dion-Bouton 24 h.p. Pl. 58

A check of buses running in London on Easter Monday 1906 revealed that of 393 motorbuses in the capital, 44 were of De Dion-Bouton manufacture, ten more than had been counted a fortnight before. The L.G.O.C. had been forced to turn to this French make for its new double-deck chassis since Milnes-Daimlers had order books overflowing. By November of that year, the De Dions had recorded their 'ton', but from then onwards progress was rather slow with approximately seven new vehicles per month being added to the tally, until the final total of 181 was arrived at by September 1908. The L.M.O.C. also purchased some De

Dions (e.g. LN 358–63), as did Birch Bros., who built their own 34-seat bodies for LC 4813 and LC 6505 in 1906. Outside the Metropolis, the Haven Hotel at Poole (Dorset) bought one in 1905 (EL 273) with an 18-seat single-deck bus body for collecting their patrons from local railway stations. They purchased a second De Dion later that year. The L.N.W.R. tried out a double-decker of this type (LC 4813 of Birch Bros.), and it was followed by the Midland Railway and the Great Northern, which also used this vehicle in a demonstration capacity, although no orders seem to have resulted from these examinations. Eastbourne Corporation in 1911 purchased no less than sixteen second-hand 24 h.p. De Dion double-deckers and numbered them as Nos. 15–30 in their growing fleet. All but the first four came from Associated of London, who had bought them new over the period 1907–10. Incidentally, whereas Nos. 19–28 received new East Sussex registrations as AP 2021/3/5/7/9/31/3/5/7/9, Nos. 29 (LC 4414) and 30 (LC 2957) retained their London marks.

As it appeared at the 1907 Olympia Show the De Dion-Bouton was powered by a four-cylinder engine with bore/stroke of 104 mm/130 mm, which developed up to 30 b.h.p. at 1,350 r.p.m. There was a plate clutch fitted. Two years later the Wigan & Chorley District Motor Bus Company ordered three of this type.

Dennis 20 h.p. Pl. 57, 97, 98

Even as early as 1905 Dennis was advertising its worm driven chassis suitable for a 34-seat double-deck body. Powered by a four-cylinder engine with a bore of 4 in. and a stroke of 5 in., this developed 20 b.h.p. at 950 r.p.m. The drive to the patent back axle was by a longitudinal shaft, and in an era when the chain drive was almost universal on commercial models the Dennis was well ahead of its time. It sold at £800. By July of that year it was being quoted at £850, but now it had a larger engine with a bore increased to 4½ in. and a stroke up to 5⅝ in., bringing it to a rating of 24 b.h.p. The wheelbase was 11 ft 6 in. Dennis themselves made rather extravagant claims for their vehicles. In 1906 in an advertisement they boasted that their buses were '50% more silent than any other bus in London' (due to the patent worm gearing) and that this method had 'six times the wearing life of any other gearing adopted'. But then with over 300 Milnes-Daimlers and the same number of Strakers-Squires running in August 1907, there were still only six Dennis buses running in London.

It may not have found any champions in London (and indeed Dennis has never flourished there much), but there were those willing to buy these interesting vehicles in the provinces. For example Mail Motors of Grimsby bought a pair in 1906. EE 312 had an orthodox double-deck body, and later became Provincial No. 1. Sister EE 313 had a front-entrance/staircase double-deck body for working as a pay-as-you-enter bus, although this was rebuilt to rear-entrance/staircase in 1912. This became No. 2 in the Provincial fleet. Belfast & County Down Railway bought two as charabancs in 1905 (OI 289 and OI 432).

Indeed it was in the sphere of the charabanc that Dennis was most successful before the First World War. Its new 40 h.p. model of 1907 with its four-cylinder engine (bore: 130 mm/stroke: 140 mm) found favour with the Llandudno Motor Car Company, which purchased six fitted with 19-seat charabanc bodies (including DB 145), whilst the Mourne Mountains Touring Company invested in one charabanc (IJ 718) and one single-decker bus (IJ 719) of this type in 1910. But with a 40 h.p. engine this Dennis could, of course, quite easily bear a 34-seat double-decker body, as Cardiff Tramways Company dis-

covered when it purchased six (BO 204–9) in 1907, followed by a further half dozen two years later.

Dennis still manufactured a smaller 20 h.p. chassis for the type of routes that the Great Western Railway used buses on as feeders to its rural train services. This was a specialist field that Dennis's kept going up to the 1930s through its Darts, Aces, Maces and Falcons. In 1911 the G.W.R. purchased ten of these little vehicles. One of them (No. 156, T 2100) was typical, being fitted with a G.W.R. body seating thirteen inside the saloon, with a further three on drop seats if necessary.

At the 1913 Olympia Show Dennis displayed its 'Subsidy' model, based on its 3-tonner commercial chassis. This was rated as a 30 h.p., and Elliott Bros. of Bournemouth bought two as 20-seat charabancs (EL 1570/1). This model sold at £810 complete. West Bridgford U.D.C. seems to have been the first municipality that took an interest in this model (in 1914).

Durham-Churchill 24 h.p.
Pl. 59, 60

At Grimesthorpe, Sheffield were manufactured the charabancs that graced many an Edwardian 'watering place'. At the 1905 Royal Agricultural Hall Show, Durham-Churchill displayed their four-cylinder 24 h.p. charabanc with its twenty bench seats. It was powered by an Aster engine (bore: 105 mm/stroke: 140 mm) rated at 30 b.h.p. at 1,000 r.p.m. It had a 14 ft 6 in. wheelbase. A Champion friction clutch was fitted and a four-speed gearbox. There was a live back axle, but this was used only for propulsion, since there was also a solid axle curved out to the rear, so as to clear the differential, and it was this that took the weight of the rear portion of the vehicle. The complete vehicle sold for £600. At the 1908 Olympia a 26-seat Durham-Churchill charabanc was shown, and this still was powered by the 30 b.h.p. Aster engine. Having managed to fit bodies seating up to 30 passengers (as in the case of SD 501, which Thomas Lees of Girvan used for carrying tourists round the shores of the Firth of Clyde), in 1908 Durham-Churchill built W 1237, a prototype 16-seater charabanc.

Not all the Durham-Churchills were employed for excursions and tours. Barton's original No. 1 (W 963) was a 20-seater of this make that inaugurated his Beeston to Nottingham route in 1908, while the Woolton Motor Omnibus Company used one for its services in the Liverpool area (K 1536). The Durham-Churchills were still going strong up to the outbreak of the First World War, for the London & South Coast Haulage Company bought ones in 1912 (CD 2031/2155), 1913 (CD 2485) and 1914 (CD 2537), and these were subsequently acquired by the newly formed South-down Motor Services in 1915.

Dürkopp 24 h.p.

In November 1905 the second most popular chassis after Milnes-Daimler for London motorbus operators was the German-built Dürkopp, imported by the Motor Car Emporium Ltd. At that time nineteen of these vehicles were on the Metropolitan streets, and their number rose to a peak of 32 the following autumn, although at one stage the London Road Car Company had placed an order for 51 (March 1905). The last of these were withdrawn in November 1908. Among those ordering this make were Provincial Carriers (ten vehicles) and the Derbyshire Motor Omnibus Company (one 22-seat single-deck bus). Hastings Omnibus Company purchased one (DY 115), as did the Great Western Railway Company. In the latter case they had a mixture of bodies and uses. For example No. 74 (CO 150) had a 19-seat charabanc body, and was used on their Plymouth to Burrator (Dartmoor) route. Its centre seats were removable and could be stored in the boot, thus converting it to a 'bus'. It had a fixed roof. On the other hand its LC 2002 was in the form of a double-decker. Another railway company, the N.E.R., bought some as single-deck buses (e.g. BT 175, SA 238). Eventually, by 1912, the N.E.R. was operating sixteen Dürkopps.

This 24 h.p. vehicle had a four-cylinder engine with bore/stroke of 150 mm/130 mm, and developed 35 b.h.p. at 1,000 r.p.m. There was a four-speed gearbox, and the final drive was by means of roller chains. One such vehicle was exhibited at the 1907 Olympia Show.

There was a second model imported into this country. This was described as an 18/20 h.p. version, and found favour in the Midlands, where not only did the Birmingham Motor Express Company buy one fitted with a 30-seat double-deck body (O 1280), but Birmingham Corporation invested in four (O 1301–4), the first two of the batch being given charabanc bodies at a later date and being re-registered as O 2898/9.

In 1909 Messrs. Pearce & Climpson of Hastings experimented with the conversion of a four-cylinder 24/30 h.p. Dürkopp engine by running it on coal gas supplied by the British Oxygen Company. It was discovered in trials that this gas, at a pressure of 120 atmospheres, gave the same mileage for every 70 cubic feet consumed as one gallon of petrol.

F.I.A.T. 24/40 h.p.

One of the continental manufacturers that made some impression on the British p.s.v. scene before the advent of the First World War was the Italian firm of F.I.A.T. In 1905 it was advertising its four-cylinder 24/40 h.p. model with its automatic lubricating system dependant on the speed of the engine. The engine was located under the driver's seat instead of in front of him. The 1907

Olympia Show had a F.I.A.T. with a four-cylinder engine with bore/stroke of 125 mm/150 mm and rated at 40 h.p. A multiple disc clutch made up of 28 bronze plates was fitted, and the final drive was by side chains. The flywheel with a diameter of 27 in. was regarded as on the large side for this period. The overall length of the chassis was 19 ft 7½ in., while its width was 7 ft 4 in. Unfortunately for this importer, the F.I.A.T. was not one of the foreign buses employed by the London-based operators. However, it did find favour in the provinces to a limited degree. One double-decker played an active part in establishing bus routes on the Isle of Wight (DL 131).

Fischer Petrol-Electric. Pl. 62

In April 1903 the L.G.O.C. took delivery of its first motorbus. This was a Fischer petrol-electric that had been imported from the United States, and had subsequently been given a double-deck body by the operators. This monstrous looking vehicle ran on an experimental service in the capital in May of that year. The petrol engine drove a dynamo, which supplied current to drive the electric motors, which in turn provided the transmission power for the rear wheels. In between the dynamo and the motors were accumulators, whose storage helped to make the whole bus rather bulky. Indeed, the Metropolitan Police at first refused to countenance it, claiming that it was far too wide. Eventually it was the heavy petrol consumption rate that caused the L.G.O.C. to abandon its trials, return the vehicle to Fischers, demand their money back (£450), and cancel the order for a further eight chassis. Indeed the General estimated that it had made a net loss of £319 during the seven months in which it ran the vehicle.

Germain 24 h.p. Pl. 63

The London Road Car Company (fleet name 'Union Jack') bought some Germain double-deckers for its routes. These were manufactured in Germany, and a 24 h.p. model was shown at the 1907 Olympia. This had a four-cylinder engine of bore/stroke 120 mm/140 mm, and developed 24 b.h.p. at 800 r.p.m. There was a multiple disc clutch, made up of no less than 80 plates and this gave a very smooth and easy drive. Transmission was through chains from the sprockets on the ends of the differential countershaft. The driver sat above the engine.

This make did not catch on in Britain, and few were imported.

Hallford-Stevens Petrol-Electric. Pl. 65

In January 1908 a new hybrid bus was given a public demonstration on the streets of Coventry. This was a petrol-electric chassis designed jointly by J. & E. Hall Ltd. of Dartford and another Kentish firm, W. A. Stevens Ltd. of Maidstone. This was by no means the first petrol-electric bus to see the light of day in this country, for in 1906 E. & H. Hora of Camberwell had built an 18-seat bus body (taking only eight days from the design stage to the completed vehicle!) for a so-called 'L'Auto Mixte' chassis produced by Messrs. Pieper of Liège. Describing this chassis, *The Commercial Motor* related that 'The motive power is derived from a petrol engine in conjunction with an electric motor. Transmission is by an electric clutch, and a cardan shaft to the back axle, which carries the differential gearing. No gearbox is used for the different speeds.' The petrol engine in question was a four-cylinder unit with a bore/stroke of 100 mm/100 mm.

Later that same year there appeared the Hart-Durtnall electric bus, which had an 'ordinary i/c engine', a small continuous-current dynamo (rated at 1½ h.p.), a polyphase multi-polar alternating current generator, a motor with a rotor to gear with the differential shaft/live back axle, and a magnetic clutch between the generator and the motor. By the beginning of 1907 an article in *The Commercial Motor* listed no less than thirteen methods of petrol-electric transmission, including one by Stevens. Later that year there appeared the Wolseley-Siddley/B.T.H. 40 h.p. petrol-electric bus, whilst the 1908 Olympia included a Greenwood-Batley petrol-electric vehicle.

Hallford had built a 3-tonner, which had won a gold medal in Class E of the 1907 R.A.C. Rally. This had a four-cylinder 110 mm/140 mm engine rated at 30/38 h.p., so it was only another step to 1908 Olympia for this manufacturer to display its 'S.B. & S.' petrol-electric bus with air compression brakes. The 30 h.p. engine ran best at 1,050 r.p.m. Each motor drove one road wheel by David Brown worm gearing to a dead axle. In 1908 the Brighton, Hove & Preston United Omnibus Company purchased one of these Hallford-Stevens chassis on to which was placed the body of CD 620. In 1910 the B.H. & P.U.O.C. bought three more, fixing on to them three of the ex-Electrobus bodies and re-registering them as CD 874/80/7. The batteries carried by these buses consisted of 48 Tudor cells, and had the capacity to cover 30 miles without recharging. Their patent back axles were designed jointly by P. Frost-Smith (Tillings), Frank Brown (David Brown) and W. A. Stevens himself, known as the S.B. & S. syndicate.

Leyland-Crossley 30 b.h.p.

Trading under its former name of Lancashire Steam Motor Company, Leyland had on view at the Royal Agricultural Hall in March 1905 a four-cylinder Crossley-engined bus with a channel steel frame. The power unit was rated at 30 b.h.p. at 1,000 r.p.m. Crossleys also supplied the automatic carburettor. A large flywheel clutch was provided and

there were two separate gear change levers for the vehicle, one operating the three forward speeds, and the other the neutral and reverse positions.

The New London & Suburban Omnibus Company ordered six of this model, while the London General purchased two Leyland-Crossleys, one of which was LC 901. Birch Brothers took delivery of one (LC 3680) in 1906, and a second one (LN 3317) the following year. Both of these buses had 34-seat double-deck bodies built by the operator.

At the Royal Agricultural Show in March 1906 the Lancashire Steam Motor Company demonstrated its more powerful 35–40 h.p. bus. This had a four-cylinder engine with a bore of $4\frac{3}{4}$ in. and a stroke of $5\frac{1}{2}$ in., developing 33 b.h.p. at 900 r.p.m. and 40 b.h.p. at 1,200 r.p.m. An aluminium cone clutch was fitted, and the transmission was by means of a prop shaft encased in a metal tube connected to a concentric back axle. Manchester Corporation put three of this model (N 1593, 1601/2) on its Northenden to Palatine Road route that year, while the New London & Suburban Omnibus Company bought one with a 34-seat rear-entrance body (P 2760). Actually, one of the demonstrators had been given a 40-seat double-deck body by Milnes-Voss of Birkenhead, and this incorporated a front staircase so that it could be used for one man working. Clacton-on-Sea Motor Omnibus Company used a 35/40 h.p. Leyland for excursion work, having a 32-seat charabanc body fitted that had a fixed roof and a glass window at its rear. The number of Leylands running on London routes remained very small during this period. In September 1907 it was merely seven, and this had only doubled by the following summer.

The 1907 Royal Agricultural Society Hall Show brought in an even more powerful model, rated at 50 h.p., which introduced the famous water dome at the top of the radiator that was a feature on Leyland chassis for the next decade. *The Commercial Motor*'s comment on this vehicle was 'Whilst unnecessarily powerful for London, (it) is eminently suitable for use on hilly country routes.'

Leyland 'X' Series. Pl. 102, 103

In 1907 Leylands introduced to the world its 'X' chassis. This was a 35 h.p. 3½-tonner, the engine of which was a 6 litre unit with a bore of 4⅝ in. and a stroke of 5½ in., developing 40 b.h.p. at 1,200 r.p.m. It was designed to take a 34-seat double-decker body. However, one of the first 'Xs' to enter service was a rear-entrance single-decker, B 2113, which was purchased by Haslingden Corporation. Later a 30-seat charabanc body was fitted to this chassis. On the other hand, Worthing Motor Services had a 39-seat Dodson double-decker body fitted to their 'X' registered DL 493. A smaller version, the X2, found favour with the Stafford Motor Service and Supply Company, who had their chassis fitted with an 18-seat Stagg & Robson body. One Leyland 'X' was fitted with the experimental Thomas Transmission System in 1909. LN 9894 was equipped with two electrical machines. These machines could operate on the shaft, so that the vehicle was propelled partly by electrical means and partly by mechanical means, or alternatively they could be operated wholly by mechanical means by using a direct drive. An epicyclic gearbox was provided. A small battery consisting of six cells was carried; this was recharged by the front dynamo. One advantage of this system was that the controller provided for a large number of running speeds, full engine power being utilized at all times. For a period of four months LN 9894 ran on behalf of Bournemouth Corporation on a route between Boscombe Arcade and Boscombe Pier, a route which involved a steep climb up from sea level. Another customer of the 'X' was Autocar of

Tunbridge Wells. In 1910 it bought three for its local routes in the Kent spa (B 2223/4/42). These machines had 32 seats, an entrance at the very rear of the vehicle, a luggage rack on the roof, and the unexpected refinement of curtains in the windows. A further three were ordered for the following year.

As from 1907 there was a larger version of the 'X', designated the 'U'. This was given a 50 h.p. engine of similar design to that of the 'X'. Amongst the patrons of the 'U' were Todmorden Corporation in 1907 with a pair of double-deckers (B 2079/82) and Keighley Corporation in 1910. Their C 4114 had a 50-seat Stagg & Robson body.

Maudslay 14 b.h.p.

It was in 1904 that the long-established engineering firm of Maudslay began to build p.s.v. chassis, albeit its first effort was to manufacture a 25 h.p. three-cylinder 6-seater bus. The following year at the 1905 Show Maudslay had on display its new two-cylinder model with bore/stroke of 5 in./3½ in., giving a capacity of 2·44 litres. An unusual feature for Edwardian commercial vehicles was Maudslay's overhead valves, operated by push rods. The four-speed gearbox included a safety catch that had to be removed before the reverse gear could be engaged. The Show bus was in the livery of the G.W.R. and was destined to enter service on its Slough to Farnham Royal route. It had an entrance at the very back of the vehicle, and was priced at £600. There were twelve seats inside the saloon, with an additional two seats beside the driver. A similar vehicle (DU 324) was built for the Winchester Public Service Omnibus Company that year.

Maudslay 30/40 h.p. Pl. 67–69

At the 1905 Olympia Show Maudslay introduced its first double-deck chassis, powered by a four-cylinder 6·44 litre engine that had equal bore/stroke of 5 in., and developed 40 b.h.p. at 750 r.p.m. The valves were operated by an overhead camshaft. The final drive was by 2 in. pitch roller chain. There was a gate gearchange employed. The Simms-Bosch high tension ignition system was used. The chassis frame was made of channel steel of cross section $4\frac{3}{4}$ in. by $2\frac{1}{2}$ in. The Show vehicle was in the livery of S.M.T., and had a 34-seat body. It was used on 1 January 1906 to inaugurate Scottish Motor Traction's first route based on Edinburgh. S 543 was followed by eight more Maudslays (S 544–51) in the initial batch, and then by a further five similar vehicles later in 1906 (S 781, S 839, S 1378/9/91). These are all quoted as having 35 seats. The first Maudslay to work in London was the London Road Car Company's LC 4136, which commenced service on 2 July 1906. Later the model was called the 35/45 h.p. and its overall length given as 18 ft $4\frac{1}{2}$ in. The number of Maudslays used in London does not seem to have risen above six. Silver Cars of Ilfracombe used the double-deck chassis for their 20-seat charabanc T 299.

In 1908 Maudslay replaced chains for final drive by an orthodox live axle. At the 1908 Olympia one of these new models was on view in the livery of the Midland Railway, and was stated to be powered by a 25/30 h.p. engine. This particular vehicle had a rear-entrance single-deck bus body, and later that year the M.R. took delivery of another (BD 745), but with a front entrance instead.

Milnes-Daimler 16 h.p.

On 27 November 1902 a great new partnership came into being in the commercial vehicle world, that between the British firm of G. F. Milnes & Co. and the German manufacturing concern Daimler Motoren-Gesellschaft. 12 April 1903 is a landmark in British p.s.v. history too, for on that day the first municipally-owned motorbus ran in Britain, when

Eastbourne Corporation inaugurated its bus service between the railway station and the district at the foot of Beachy Head known as Meads. Milnes-Daimlers Nos. 1–4 (later registered as AP 291/3/5/89) had 14-seat front-entrance bodies, but were given new 20-seat saloon bodies three years later. On 17 August 1903 yet another milestone was reached when the first motorbus owned by a railway company entered service between Helston and the Lizard, run by the G.W.R. The vehicle used was, of course, a Milnes-Daimler 16 h.p. and in this instance bore a 22-seat waggonette-style body. It was acquired second-hand from Sir George Newnes, who had worked it in association with the Lynton & Barnstaple Railway, a narrow-gauge line which he had sponsored.

At the 1905 Show one of these smaller Milnes-Daimlers was on display. This had a four-cylinder engine with a bore/stroke of 100 mm/130 mm, developing 18 b.h.p. at 800 r.p.m. With a wheelbase of 10 ft 6 in., the chassis had an overall width of 6 ft 6 in. There was a cone clutch and four-speed gearbox. Three brakes were fitted (gear shaft, rear wheels surface, drums on the differential cross shaft).

The G.W.R. brought several of these vehicles, which are sometimes listed as 20 h.p. AF 38 and CO 141 were charabancs on the company's popular tourist excursion from Penzance to Land's End; AF 80 had a 34-seat double-deck body; AF 141 was a 20-seater single-decked bus. The Birmingham Motor Express Company bought half-a-dozen of these chassis in 1904, and had 34-seat double-deck bodies fitted to O 264–9. In March 1907 O 264/7 were given charabanc bodies instead and re-registered as O 2619/20. Eastbourne Corporation continued to patronise this model with purchases of 20 h.p. double-deckers in 1903 (No. 6), 1904 (No. 8), 1905 (No. 9) and 1906 (Nos. 10–14, AP 2009/11/13/17/19). Perhaps one of the more unusual purchases was that of LC 3621 by one Charles Frohman, who bought this single-decker to give free rides to play-goers at Hicks Theatre, where it earned the title of 'Monty Brewster's Motor Bus'.

Milnes-Daimler 24 h.p. Pl. 70–73

At the Crystal Palace Motor Show in February 1904 Milnes-Daimler (of Hadley, Salop) exhibited a 24 h.p. double-decker on a chassis with the following dimensions:

wheelbase : 10 ft 3½ in.
overall length : 16 ft 3½ in.
width : 6 ft 6 in.
diameter, front wheels : 32 in.
diameter, rear wheels : 42 in.

This prototype went to Hastings & St. Leonards Omnibus Company (DY 84), which ran it on its route between Bo-Peep and Alexandra Park. Later that year a second Milnes-Daimler double-decker (DY 96) joined it. Further along the Sussex coast the Brighton, Hove & Preston United Omnibus Company in 1904 bought two (CD 103 and CD 236) with Birch 34-seat bodies, followed by a further pair (CD 620/665) in 1906, this time with bodies constructed by the operators. Continuing westwards, the Worthing Motor Omnibus Company bought at least three double-deckers for both its town routes and for the service into Brighton (BP 311, CD 335 and CD 361), these having 36-seat bodies. But it was the entry into service in London of Thomas Tilling's first Milnes-Daimler (A 6934) on 30 September 1904 that clinched the success of this model. This operator soon had thirteen more on its routes, including A 8215/16, A 8649/50, A 8759, A 9175 and LC 973. Birch Bros. followed suit almost immediately (11 October), building their own 34-seat bodies for A 7045/6, A 8545, LC 1043, LC 3160, LC 5476, LC 6193, LC 7590

and LC 7743, delivered over a period of two years. On 27 March 1905 the London Motor Omnibus Company ('Vanguard') brought into service its first five Milnes-Daimlers. One of these (A 9129) was used on a new daily express route during August that year between London and Brighton, and this vehicle was soon joined by a second vehicle of this type (LC 2823), which although it had a rear positioned staircase, also had a front door to the lower saloon! On 29 May 1905 the mighty London General Omnibus Company placed into active service its first Milnes-Daimler double-deckers (LC 3725–30). By November that year 81 Milnes-Daimlers were running in the capital, and this figure had passed the 100 mark early the next year. There were 200 such buses operating in London by July 1906, and 300 by May 1907. Thereafter the pace slackened and a peak of 322 was achieved in October of that year.

By the 1905 Show the chassis had been lengthened to an overall 19 ft 6 in., with a wheelbase of 13 ft. The chassis was 2 ft 10 in. above the ground. Another improvement was that the lower half of the crank chamber had been dropped, so that the big end bearings could be got out without the entire engine having to be dismantled, as had been necessary with the earlier versions. The engine used in the 1905 model was a four-cylinder unit with a bore/stroke of 110 mm/140 mm rated at 28–30 b.h.p. at 800 r.p.m.

In October 1906 details were released of a new 28 h.p. model, in which the overall chassis length had been further increased to 19 ft 11 in., although the wheelbase dimensions remained the same. The four-cylinder engine had bore/stroke of $4\frac{5}{16}$ in./$5\frac{1}{2}$ in. and the optimum revs were 850 r.p.m. Instead of the chassis members being made from rolled channel steel, they were now assembled from pressed steel. Commenting on the one shown at the 1907 Olympia, *The*

Commercial Motor reporter commented that it was 'a splendid example of high class workmanship'.

The G.W.R. had shown an interest in the 24 h.p. model, having some of them fitted with 34-seat double-deck bodies (e.g. AF 188 and AF 278) and others with 26-seat charabanc bodywork (e.g. T 490), while yet others served as 19-seat single-deck buses (e.g. T 494). Now, in 1907, the L.N.W.R. bought one of the new 28 h.p. Milnes-Daimlers as a double-decker (LN 3850), and this was equipped with a special luggage compartment with double doors on the front nearside of the vehicle. The Lancashire & Yorkshire Railway Company also purchased a double-decker (B 2084). The Great Western used one of these 28 h.p. models on its Llandyssil Station to New Quay route, using the top deck of EJ 37 for parcels and luggage, instead of fitting seats for passengers! The Isle of Wight Express Motor Syndicate between 1905 and 1907 took delivery of fourteen of this make (including DL 75). The Sussex Motor Road Car Company pioneered a new coastal route between Bognor and Portsmouth in October 1907 using a double-decked Milnes-Daimler (CD 408), whilst *The Commercial Motor* itself employed another double-decker (LN 5852) to cover the R.A.C. 1,000 mile Commercial Rally of September/October 1907. Bath Electric Tramways Company bought five with 32-seat Dodson bodies (FB 02–07) for their Bathford feeder routes.

One L.G.O.C. vehicle was experimentally fitted with a Dennis live axle and worm drive in place of its chains during April 1907.

Moss & Woodd 'Orion'. Pl. 74

On 16 December 1904, the L.G.O.C. introduced a rather strange looking double-decker (A 8010) that had a 26-seat horse-bus type body with the upper deck extended over the driver's seat (an unusual practice at this time). The 16-h.p. chassis had been imported from Switzerland by Messrs. Moss & Woodd, and was known as the 'Orion'. It was withdrawn in February 1906. The Victoria Omnibus Company followed suit, and took the lion's share of Orions as far as London was concerned, with vehicles like Nos. 35 (LC 1767) and 36 (LC 2370). The first went into service on 23 August 1905. These four-cylinder buses had only 20 h.p. engines, yet were designed to carry 34-seat double-deck bodies. Their final drive was by means of side chains, and a four-speed gearbox was provided. In October 1906 Moss & Woodd announced an improved version of the Orion, which was now powered by a new vertical four-cylinder engine of bore/stroke 130 mm/150 mm and rated at 40 b.h.p. at 900 r.p.m., compared with the former horizontal engine of 160 mm/180 mm bore/stroke that had developed only 25 b.h.p. at 900 r.p.m. The new Orion had a cone clutch and a gated four-speed gearbox, the transmission being by means of Renold roller chains. During 1906 only 11 Orions were licensed for operating in London, and by July of the following year they had all been withdrawn.

Cambrian Railways purchased a pair of the smaller two-cylinder 16 h.p. Orions for their Pwllheli to Nefyn route. Nos. 1/2 (CC 162/3) sat 22 passengers and had two doors. Two people could sit next to the driver, eight in the forward enclosed saloon, and the remaining twelve in the rear saloon.

The Moss and Woodd partnership was dissolved on 31 December 1907.

Motor Omnibus Construction

This Walthamstow factory, a subsidiary of the Vanguard group of bus companies, assembled parts manufactured by other firms during 1906. For example, the engines were supplied by R. Hornsby & Sons of Grantham, and were four-cylinder units with a bore/stroke of 110 mm/140 mm, developing 32 b.h.p. at 900 r.p.m. Armstrong Whitworth sent the axles. The M.O.C. chassis was provided with a cone clutch and a four-speed gearbox. Eight of these vehicles were to be seen on the streets of London, but they were withdrawn in September 1907.

Nevertheless, in April 1909 London General used a special M.O.C. chassis, which had been experimentally fitted with Crompton electrical driving equipment. Electric Power Storage Company accumulators weighing 37 cwt were connected to two $7\frac{1}{2}$ h.p. motors mounted one each side of the chassis, the drive being taken from each motor to a separately hung countershaft by high speed silent chains. This increased the unladen weight of the vehicle from $4\frac{1}{2}$ tons to 6 tons 7 cwt, so that it fell outside the requirements laid down by the Metropolitan Police.

The later work of the Walthamstow factory forms part of the A.E.C.-L.G.O.C. story.

Napier 35 h.p.

The first Napier used for bus work was an open waggonette seating seven, which was licensed on 14 April 1902 to the Pioneer Omnibus Co. of Brondesbury to operate along the Edgware Road between Marble Arch and Cricklewood. In 1906, there emerged from Napier's works in Acton Vale on the western periphery of London a four-cylinder-engined chassis with equal bore/stroke of 5 in. The overall chassis frame length was 18 ft $10\frac{5}{8}$ in., with a width of 3 ft 8 in. and a ground clearance of 2 ft $4\frac{1}{2}$ in. The wheelbase measured 12 ft. There was a friction plate clutch and a three-speed gearbox. However, the Napier did not find favour with the London operators, and it was to be several years before a newer model appeared, a model which commanded more respect, and led to quite a successful run for the ensuing decade.

Scheibler 35/40 h.p.

These German-built chassis from Aachen first arrived in 1905 for the London Motor Omnibus Company, and by the following year there were fourteen of them bearing the legend 'Vanguard' on their flanks. One of these, A 9141, fitted with a 34-seat Bayleys double-decked body, was used by the L.M.O.C. on its London to Brighton express service. This particular model of the Scheibler had a four cylinder engine with a bore/stroke of 120 mm/140 mm and was fitted with a four-speed gearbox. The final drive was by means of Hans Renold side chains.

At the 1907 Olympia Show Scheibler exhibited a smaller vehicle driven by a two-cylinder engine and possessing a three-speed gearbox. Again the final drive was by way of side chains. No important patrons for this were found in this country.

Scott-Stirling 14 h.p.

When the London Motor Omnibus Syndicate reorganised itself as the London Power Omnibus Company (using the fleet name 'Pioneer') early in 1904, it decided to use Scott-Stirling chassis built by its associated company at Twickenham. By August 1906 there were 25 of this make on the streets of London, and this total rose to 67 by June of the following year. Then on 16 July 1907 they were all withdrawn from service, as were many other makes, due largely to the more exacting requirements of the Metropolitan Police that came into effect in April 1907.

The two-cylinder Scott-Stirling had a bore/stroke of $4\frac{5}{8}$ in./$5\frac{1}{2}$ in. and developed 14 b.h.p. at 750 r.p.m. Transmission was by way of a bevel crown drive. In March 1906 the model on view bore an 18-seat rear-entrance single-deck bus body, such as the London Power Omnibuses had employed a year earlier. One, in the form of a 22-seat charabanc, appeared at the 1907 Show.

The larger version of the Scott-Stirling had a 24 h.p. engine and was shown in 1906 as a 36-seat double-decker, with a distinctive double radiator in the front. This was the prototype for Pioneer's 34-seaters, such as LC 2613–8, which shortly afterwards entered service in London. Compared with Dennis, Milnes-Daimler and Commer, the Scott-Stirling remained one of the lesser known makes of p.s.v. chassis. The Cambridge Omnibus Company did buy two buses for its Market Hill to Chesterton route.

In April 1908 it was announced that the firm had gone into liquidation.

Straker-Squire-Büssing 24 h.p.

Pl. 77, 78

By the beginning of 1906 there were 51 of this type of bus working in London, the first having entered service with the L.R.C.C. on 6 March 1905. By May of that year they had topped the century, and a further 100 were added by October. The 300 mark was passed in July 1907, and two months later the Straker-Squire-Büssings overtook Milnes-Daimlers as the most popular motorbus in London, eventually reaching a plateau of 366 in October 1908. The G.W.R. invested in some with a variety of bodies. For example, No. 78 (AF 161) had a 20-seat charabanc body, while its sister No. 79 (AF 160) had a Scammell 40-seat front-entrance/staircase double-deck body. Another G.W.R. Straker-Squire operated between Torquay and Brixham (T 586) and had a 26-seat charabanc body with a fixed roof. Bath Electric Tramways took delivery of a batch of six with 35-seat double-deck bodywork constructed by the Bristol Wagon & Carriage Works Company (FB 08–13) for use on their feeder routes from the Bathford tram terminus.

The engine in this model was of four cylinders with bore/stroke dimensions of 105 mm/130 mm, developing 24 b.h.p. at 950 r.p.m. The gearbox was equipped with no less than six forward speeds and two reverse speeds. A prop shaft helped to carry the transmission to two roller chains. This model sold at £850. In November 1905 improvements were announced which involved the frame being widened at the rear from 3 ft 3½ in. to 3 ft 9½ in., and brought 5 in. nearer to the ground. New 12-leaf springs 52 in. long were fitted to the rear, and the gearbox was moved closer to the clutch.

In 1907 a new engine was fitted to the Straker-Squire, being of four cylinders, but this time with equal 5 in. bore and stroke, and developing 30 b.h.p. The clutch was described in *The Commercial Motor* at the time of the 1907 Olympia as being 'novel: one of the simplest adjustments yet seen. The clutch fork is vertical, and the central fulcrum is in the form of a jaw: this jaw is at the outer end of a screwed portion, which is adjustable in a bracket bolted to a transverse member carrying the clutch-pedal mountings. The upper end of the clutch fork is provided with a vertical roller which lies between two small lugs.'

At the same time Straker-Squire produced a petrol-electric chassis, fitted with the standard 30 b.h.p. engine, a dynamo (an armature rotated directly from the engine crankshaft) supplying current to two continuous-current motors, which drove two short secondary shafts by worm gearing, the final drive being by side chains. However, with several other petrol-electrics appearing, this model did not meet with as much success as its more orthodox stable-mate.

By 1911 Straker-Squire was producing the improved 'U' type of double-deck chassis. Worthing Motor Services took delivery of one (DL 621) fitted with a Dodson 36-seat body, while the Great Eastern London Motor Omnibus Company did likewise (AN 989). The Brighton, Hove & Preston United Omnibus Company tried out a pair of 'U' chassis fitted with 30-seat charabanc bodywork

(CD 1441/1681). Since 1907 the Straker-Squires had had more powerful 40 h.p. engines, and these had been fitted to the buses operated by the London Road Car Company (e.g. LN 211–21) and London General (e.g. LN 290–8). These were also given Morse silent chains for the final drive to the rear axle.

Thames Ironworks 35/40 h.p.

In 1906 the Thames Iron Works, Ship-building and Engineering Co. Ltd., based on the bank of the Thames at Green-wich, was producing a *six*-cylinder-engined chassis with a bore of 4½ in. and a stroke of 6 in., which developed 50 b.h.p. at 900 r.p.m. The London & South Coast Motor Services purchased some of these powerful machines in that year for express coach routes. One of these, D 2449, had a 19-seat charabanc body, which was most unusual in that eight of these passengers could sit in an enclosed rear section. Others were registered FN 503/6/14. They were noted for their large diameter driving wheels, which measured 4 ft 4 in. across.

In addition, in 1906 the company was producing a four-cylinder 24/30 h.p. model, suitable for carrying a 36-seat double-deck body. Its maximum speed was, however, stated to be only 14 m.p.h., which although above that permitted in towns did not leave much room for challenge. This model also appeared at the 1907 Olympia Show, where its bore/stroke dimensions were given as 4¾ in./5½ in. developing 40 b.h.p. at 850 r.p.m. A four-speed gearbox was fitted and a leather faced cone clutch. The overall chassis length was 19 ft 1 in., giving a wheelbase of 12 ft 6 in. and a width of 7 ft. In spite of its localised name, none of the London operators seemed to be interested in this bus.

By the time we reach 1910 the Thames Iron Works was concentrating on 40 h.p. coaches, this time driven by four-cylinder engines. The final drive remained through roller chains to both rear wheels, which continued to be of considerable size (in this case 48 in. in diameter, compared with 36 in. for the front wheels). One Hastings operator ordered eight of this version fitted with 27-seat body-work.

Thornycroft 24 b.h.p. Pl. 79

The 36-seat Thornycroft 24 b.h.p. was powered by a four-cylinder engine with bore/stroke dimensions of 4½ in./5 in. and rated at 24 b.h.p. at 900 r.p.m. The wheelbase was 12 ft 9 in. and the final drive was by chains. The petrol tank held eighteen gallons, sufficient for 75 miles on 'fair roads'. In 1905 this model was selling at £900. The London Motor Omnibus Company had one of these vehicles in 1904 (O 1279), and leased it to the Birmingham Motor Express Company, who itself had a small fleet of these Thornycrofts (O 269 and O 1272–78/80). As well as O 1279, Vanguard also ran H 1936, A 9117, A 9131 and A 9142, which were part of a batch of 30 such buses. However, by September 1907 only one Thornycroft remained in service within the Metropolitan Police area. Other operators using this early Thorny-croft included Manchester District (whose ten double-deckers of this make included N 1368/9), Nottingham Corporation (AU 186), Bristol Tramways (with twelve, including AE 723 and AE 731), and Musselburgh Electric Tram-ways. In the latter case a 19-seat chara-banc body was fitted to the 24 b.h.p. chassis.

At the 1908 Olympia Thornycroft exhibited two of its new 30 h.p. chassis. One was in the livery of the L.S.W.R. and bore a 14-seat body to be used on the Exeter to Chagford route (presumably to replace the Clarkson steamer), while the second vehicle had a 29-seat chara-banc body. The Llandudno Coaching & Carriage Company ordered four of these 30 h.p. chassis, known as the 'C' model, and had local Roberts charabanc bodies attached to them.

Turgan 24 b.h.p.

In 1905 one of the French imported buses that could be seen in London was the Turgan. Balls Bros. operated some of these buses with their four-cylinder engine with equal bore/stroke of 110 mm. This developed 24 b.h.p. at 1,000 r.p.m., rising to 30 b.h.p. at 1,200 r.p.m., quite a strong unit for this date. There was a leather-covered cone clutch, which was connected to a transverse differential shaft. There was a cranked rear axle to enable the floor level to be lowered. The driver was positioned over the engine. The first British-bought Turgan was given a 34-seat double-deck body by Dodson.

Wolseley 24 b.h.p. Pl. 80

In 1905 the Wolseley Tool & Motor Car Company, to give it its full title, introduced a new range of bus chassis, suitable for fitting with 36-seat double-deck bodywork. There was a choice of two power units, both horizontally mounted. The first developed 20 b.h.p. at 750 r.p.m., while the more powerful was rated at 24 b.h.p. at the same engine speed. The bore was $4\frac{1}{2}$ in., the stroke 6 in. The chassis dimensions were: length = 15 ft 6 in.; wheelbase = 10 ft 6 in.; width (maximum) = 7 ft 2 in.; height of frame from ground = 2 ft 7 in. The final drive was by means of Hans Renold silent roller chains.

The London Motor Omnibus Company opted for the 24 b.h.p. engine for its vehicles such as A 9118, which due to Metropolitan Police regulations could only seat 34 passengers. However, Wolverhampton Corporation's trio DA 108–10 were fitted with the 20 b.h.p. unit and they too seated 34. Examples of 36-seaters were Birmingham Motor Express Company's O 1281/2, which had the smaller engine. In the Bradford region the Silsden Motor Omnibus Com-

pany purchased one of the 20 b.h.p. models (AK 640).

During 1906 a more powerful Wolseley-Siddeley 30 h.p. was placed on the market. Its four-cylinder engine had the same size bore as its predecessor, but the stroke was reduced to 5 in. It was expected to develop 33 b.h.p. at 1,050 r.p.m. Among the modifications that were included was a short propeller shaft. It was fitted with a four-speed gearbox.

This version found favour with the G.W.R., which was rapidly expanding its feeder services at this time. One was fitted with a Dodson 34-seat body, which had the unusual combination of a central entrance door to the 14-seat lower saloon and a rear staircase. Between these was included a luggage compartment. In May 1907 one of these vehicles was employed by the Great Western for Whitsuntide holiday tours of Devon and Cornwall, and later in that season went to Ireland, via Fishguard. The London General tried out the demonstrator BK 257. Although the L.G.O.C. did buy a number of this 'H' class (e.g. LN 4502), the Wolseley came a poor fourth on the streets of London, reaching a peak with 77 of this make in the summer of 1908, compared with 355 Straker-Squires, 312 Milnes-Daimlers and 169 De Dion-Boutons at that date, but it at least had the distinction of being the leading British-built chassis there.

The main influx of Wolseleys on to the London routes started in December 1907, and these were presumably the improved 35 h.p. models introduced in September of that year. These four-cylinder buses had an increased output rated at 30 b.h.p. at 1,000 r.p.m. The final drive was by roller chains. One of these chassis was given an experimental 40 h.p. B.T.H. petrol-electric motor, and went on trial with the L.G.O.C. under the trade plate ACK 2 from 18 August until Christmas Eve 1907, during which time it covered

10,480 miles. This could have been increased, but for 1,849 miles lost due to electrical faults and a further 1,061 miles never run owing to mechanical trouble. However, we must remember that at this time most buses spent a good deal of time over the pits for some reason or another. The motors were fitted rigidly to the longitudinal main frame members. The armatures were connected, through Oldham couplings, to the two worm shafts. Each of these worm shafts drove a short counter shaft, also secured to a longitudinal main frame member. The outer ends of these were provided with chain sprockets, the teeth of which were cast to take Hans Renold centre-guided silent chains. On the inner ends were keyed substantial brake-drums, which had large frictional surfaces. This advanced model does not seem to have met with much success, and at the 1908 Olympia Show Wolseley showed instead an 18 h.p. rear-entrance single-decker in the livery of the Midland Railway Company.

SECTION V: PETROL/PETROL-ELECTRIC 1910-1919

A.E.C.-L.G.O.C. 'B'. Pl. 81-85

It was in 1906 that the London Motor Omnibus Company ('Vanguard') syarted a factory at Walthamstow for the manufacture of vehicles under the name of the Motor Omnibus Construction Company, as we saw earlier. Thus, when the L.G.O.C. amalgamated with Vanguard, it also acquired these premises. On 12 August 1909 the first of the experimental 'X' class was driven out of the factory, which was now being run by the L.G.O.C. to produce a standardised vehicle which could replace all their Milnes-Daimlers, Straker-Squires, Wolseleys and other assorted makes. X1 (LC

7371) entered public service on 16 December in that year, and was followed by a further 60 double-decker buses. X1 and X2 (LC 7372) ran on the Putney to Plaistow route to begin with. These X class buses were themselves replaced by the 'B' class that evolved from them and then found homes elsewhere. For example, G. Town of Worthing purchased X59 (LN 9967) which by that time had been upseated to 36. He bought a second one (X30, LN 4588) to replace his other horse bus on the local town service at Worthing. In 1918 these two buses became Nos. 90 and 91 in the growing Southdown fleet.

Between March and 7 October 1910, work proceeded on the manufacture of B1, the first of no less than 2,900. The B was powered by a four-cylinder engine with a bore of 110 mm and a stroke of 140 mm, developing 35 b.h.p. at 1,000 r.p.m. There were 'T' head side-valves, magneto ignition and thermo-syphon cooling. A cone clutch and a separately mounted four-speed silent-chain gearbox were fitted. Transmission was by way of an open shaft to a massive worm-gear fully-floating live rear axle. Dual solid tyres were fitted to the rear axle. Later buses had the bore increased to 115 mm, and this raised the b.h.p. to 42. The overall chassis length was 19 ft 2¼ in., and the wheelbase 12 ft 10⅝ in. The body dimensions were 22 ft 6½ in. × 6 ft 10 in. The chassis weight varied from 2 tons 5 cwt to 2½ tons. The 'B' replaced many of the old horse-bus routes. For instance in October 1910 the new L.G.O.C. route 25 (Old Ford–Victoria) ousted the old horse buses named 'Old Ford' and 'Royal Blue', and was worked by nine of the 'B' class. By July 1911 the 'B' was coming off the production line at the rate of twenty per week, so that by the next month the L.G.O.C. reported that they had only 94 horse buses left operating. Not all the 'B' chassis received the 34-seat double-deck body. For example, when the rail strike took place in March 1912, twelve B type chassis fitted with lorry bodies were used to collect supplies from all over Britain (e.g. B731, LF 9402). Another (B1354, LE 9416) was given a 27-seat charabanc body, and was used for sight seeing trips.

In 1912 the L.G.O.C. separated legally its bus operating and vehicle building sides, the latter becoming known as the Associated Equipment Company (i.e. A.E.C.). By October 1912 the 'B' was really being mass-produced, at a rate of 30 chassis per week. In order to prevent any other operator from buying a 'B' and operating it in the London area, London General insisted on A.E.C. imposing a ban for a 30-mile radius calculated from the centre of London on all sales of the new bus to other operators. Indeed, this was taken so far that among the 37 B.E.T. operators who were induced to sign the agreement was one as far away as Gateshead. Some of the 'B's entered the ranks of London General's subsidiaries. Thus 55 were run on Associated Omnibus Company routes, while the Metropolitan Steam Omnibus Company replaced its Darracq-Serpollets by new 'B's. The 'B' enabled the L.G.O.C. to extend its activities right into the countryside surrounding the capital. In July 1912 it opened up route 62 to Slough and Windsor on Sundays; the first through bus was B 202 (LC 3840). A month later route 84 vetween Golders Green and St. Albans was commenced. By 1913 the 2,500 mark had been reached. Indeed in November of that year experiments were carried out for safety, since the B stood so high off the ground, and B 2662 was the vehicle chosen to have seven-barred lifeguards fitted to its sides to prevent people from falling underneath the chassis.

When the First World War broke out the War Department took delivery of no less than 300 'B's as troop carriers, while a further 300 were used in defence work

in London itself. Some of these took the form of the famous 'lorry-buses' (e.g. LU 8035/41).

Some of the 'B's were given single-deck bus bodies with rear entrances, and one of these (B 214, LA 9802) of 1910 has been preserved. Some other operators, well away from the Metropolis, bought 'B's, and we find United Automobile having one (No. A105, AH 0602) in its Norfolk-based fleet. Liverpool Corporation took delivery of one (K 1582), while one bearing a charabanc body ended up in the fleet of Bournemouth & District as its No. 4 (FX 4626). Eventually B class serial numbers reached the figure 5015 (LU 8011), since which time 4825 has been the highest figure reached by a London class (RT).

Albion 3-tonner. Pl. 86

In 1910 Albion introduced its 3-ton chassis powered by a four-cylinder engine (bore: $4\frac{1}{2}$ in.; stroke: 5 in.), rated at 32·4 h.p. A Murray governor was fitted, and this assumed command of all running speeds from 250 r.p.m. up to 1,050 r.p.m. A large diameter cone clutch was an alternative to a standard clutch with a single disc. The overall length of the chassis was 19 ft 6 in., with a wheelbase of 13 ft 1 in., and the height of the frame above the ground was 2 ft $8\frac{3}{4}$ in. The chassis weighed 42 cwt.

To pair with the 3-tonner, a 2-tonner appeared at the 1913 Olympia Show. This model, designated the A12 by Albions, had a four-cylinder engine of the same dimensions as that for the larger chassis, but rated at 25 h.p. The single-plate clutch was fitted, and a parallel form of worm drive was installed to drive the differential cross-shaft. Wolverhampton, obviously liking their two 16 h.p. vehicles, bought four of these 2-tonners in 1914, and had Roberts 24-seat front-entrance bodies fitted on to Nos. 3–6 (DA 1350–3). Meanwhile, neighbouring

West Bromwich Corporation also took delivery of a quartet of A12s, this time having 25-seat front entrance bus bodies given to EA 300–3 by the local coachbuilding firm of W. J. Smith.

Austin 2/3 tonner. Pl. 87

Towards the close of 1912 Herbert Austin introduced his commercial 2/3 ton chassis. This was powered by a four-cylinder engine with a bore/stroke of 89 mm/127 mm, and consisted mainly of parts from his 20 h.p. cars. There were, however, several new features about this particular model. For instance, the final drive was by way of dual propeller shafts, both shafts coming from a common differential unit housed behind the gearbox. Each shaft drove one of the rear wheels through a crown-wheel and pinion. The rear wheels themselves were mounted on tubular dead axles. Secondly, there was a rear-positioned radiator under the front bonnet. Thirdly, the gear lever was placed in a central position, and not on the driver's right-hand side. It was to be another fifteen years before this innovation was taken up on any large scale by vehicle manufacturers. In 1917 a more powerful engine (still rated at 20 h.p.) with an increased bore of 95 mm was fitted to the 2/3 ton Austin. In all over 2,500 of this chassis were produced, many of them going into the growing ranks of British Army transport.

In 1914 Flights, the famous Birmingham tours firm, bought an Austin 2/3 tonner (OB 4812), and had a 14-seat charabanc body fitted to it. Down in Cornwall, the Harris Bus Company had a 19-seat toast-rack body built for its AF 879 in 1916. The City of Oxford Electric Tramways Company seem to have used an Austin 2/3 tonner as a double-decker in 1915, for FC 1636 was given a 34-seat L.G.O.C. body, although one would have thought this chassis was rather underpowered to receive a double-decker body at this date.

Bellhaven 51/60 cwt

In June 1909 the Scottish manufacturer Bellhaven launched its bus chassis, described as a 51–60 cwt, and suitable for carrying a 30-seat body. The chassis length was only 15 ft 6 in., and it seemed rather underpowered, with a two-cylinder Aster engine quoted as being in the range 20–26 h.p. This unit had a bore of 5⅛ in. and a stroke of 5½ in. The model incorporated a covered metal cone clutch, and the final drive was by means of Coventry Chain Company 'Wormo' roller chains.

The Bellhaven seems to have stayed mainly in Scotland, and one of its first patrons was the British Motor Express Company of Wishaw, which bought one (V 773), and equipped it with a charabanc body. The only municipality interested in the Bellhaven appears to have been Perth Corporation, which bought one in 1911, and fitted it with a Dundee Industrial Motor Company bus body, and then used it until 1914 on a feeder service in connection with its tram routes.

Bristol 28 h.p.

The Bristol Tramways & Carriage Company began to manufacture buses at its Brislington Depot in August 1907, and by May of the following year a 16-seater of its own design was operating on a route at Clifton. By 1909 the company had started to construct bus chassis at its Filton Depot. Then in 1913 it produced its first real break-through with a four-cylinder engine chassis (bore: 4¼ in. stroke: 5 in.) rated at 28 h.p. The final drive was by worm. An unusual feature for this period was that both the gear lever and the hand brake were situated in the centre of the chassis on the driver's right-hand side. On this occasion Bristol fitted a 22-seat single-deck bus body on to the prototype 28 h.p. vehicle. One of the first municipal operators of the Bristol was Middlesbrough Corporation in 1913.

Commer W.P. Series. Pl. 92

In 1911 Commer Cars introduced the very successful W.P. Series of p.s.v. chassis. The largest of these was the WP1, later nicknamed the 'Bognor', perhaps because one of the first clients was Davies of Bognor, who took into stock three (BK 2237/45/99) with Bailey 30-seat charabanc bodies. The WP1 was originally planned as a 36-seat vehicle and was powered by a 30 h.p. engine. Indeed the demonstrator BM 1088 had a charabanc body of this capacity, as did BM 1605, which was sold to an operator in Littlehampton.

The WP2 had originally the same power unit as the WP1, but was designed to carry between 23 and 29 passengers. By 1912 this had developed into a 36 h.p. vehicle with a Linley patent gearbox and enclosed side chains, and at the Scottish Show in Glasgow in January of that year a WP2 was exhibited with a 'torpedo'-style 28-seat charabanc body. The model soon acquired the name 'Kerry', since one of the first customers was Tourist Development (Ireland) Ltd., which bought two WP2s (BM 1270 and BM 1606). A rarer body was that fitted to No. 9 in the fleet of Commercial Car Hirers, a Scammell bus body seating 23, but with a central entrance.

The smallest of the trio, the WP3, had a 22 h.p. engine, and unlike its sisters had a worm drive instead of chains. It had only a three-speed gearbox. It was planned as a 14-seater, and was shortly christened the 'Windermere'. At the 1912 Scottish Show it was announced by Commers that David MacBrayne had ordered six of this type. Lord Lonsdale purchased one fitted with a 15-seat charabanc body for use on his estate, and fortunately we can still enjoy the sight of BM 2856 at rallies. A new operator calling itself T.A.N. started a route between Andover and Tidworth in 1911 using a pair of WP3s with 14-seat Hora bus bodies.

Daimler CC Series. Pl. 61, 93–96, 109

In November 1910 B.S.A. launched a revitalised Daimler Company, based on Coventry. From its factory there issued during the second decade of this century large numbers of p.s.v. chassis, some of which were built in conjunction with A.E.C., then of Walthamstow. The key to the success enjoyed by Daimlers over this period was probably in their adoption of the American designed 'Silent Knight' engine of K. P. Knight of Wisconsin. This was a four-cylinder sleeve valve engine with a bore/stroke of 110 mm/150 mm, rated at 40 h.p. The cylinders were cast separately. A Ferodo-lined cone clutch was fitted and a chain driven gearbox. Worm drive was provided for the rear axle. The chassis of the CC model was first displayed at the 1912 Royal Agricultural Show at Doncaster, and soon a 34-seat double-decker demonstrator (DU 6552) was 'doing the rounds'. The first really big order for one type of motorbus resulted from this, when Metropolitan Electric Tramways ordered 300 chassis at £825 apiece. Gearless Motor Omnibus placed twenty into service on their route 13 (London Bridge to Golders Green), while the British Automobile Traction Co. Ltd. were receiving the CC at a rate of six per week during the autumn of 1912 for their Victoria to Liverpool Street route. W. R. Morris started up his Oxford Motor Omnibus Company with seven Daimler CC chassis bearing L.G.O.C. 34-seat bodies in 1913 (DU 4240/1/77 and DU 4313/4/8/9), and the City of Oxford Electric Tramways Company had a similar batch of twenty double-deckers (registered between DU 4197 and DU 4848). Sheffield Corporation began its first motorbus service with four Daimler CCs with 36-seat double-deck bodies (W 3201–4), whilst Worthing Motor Services purchased one (IB 707) fitted with a 42-seat Dodson body. In Grimsby the Provincial Tramways Company bought two as charabancs (Nos. 8/9, EE 758/9) and Aldershot & District had some with rear-entrance single-deck bodywork (AA 5164–7). E. Hewer of Leamington Spa built an *all steel* body on a CC chassis (DU 1830).

A modified form known as the CD (with protected magneto, cast oil tray and anti-vibrator) found favour with operators such as Potteries with their single-deck buses Nos. 1/6/12/2/10/9 (EH 489–94) and 7/4 (EH 577/8). The Barrow-in-Furness branch of the B.E.T. purchased two CDs as 24-seat charabancs (EO 578/9), whilst Gateshead Tramways bought one (J 2337) as a double-decker. In Wales Wrexham & District Tramways invested in one (CA 1040) with a Birch 26-seat single-deck bus body. Both the CC and the CD had sloping dumb irons and frames similar to the A.E.C. 'B' type.

A smaller version of the CC, known as the CB found favour at seaside resorts. For example at Cleethorpes, Provincial used CB for its Nos. 10 (EE 900) and 11 (EE 901) with 18- and 15-seat charabanc bodies respectively. In Sussex, Worthing Motor Services had charabancs on CB chassis with a variety of bodywork by B.H. & P.U.O.C. (IB 701/2), Harrington (IB 703), Dodson (IB 708), Hora (IB 709/10) and W.M.S. itself (CD 3321). At Bournemouth Elliott Bros. invested in four charabancs based on CB chassis, viz. EL 2000/1, EL 2200 and EL 2300.

The wartime version known as the 'Y' was bought in fair numbers by Birmingham Corporation. Their Nos. 41–6 (OB 1569–74) and 47–9 (OB 2101–3) had Dodson 33-seat double-deck bodies, whilst Nos. 50–8 (OB 2104–12) had 34-seat Brush bodies. The City of Oxford had Brush 32-seat single-deck rear entrance bodies fitted to a pair of Ys bought in 1916 (Nos. 33/2, FC 2195/6), following this up with a repeat order of six in 1919 (which ousted an equal number of 'DU' registered CCs, taking

over their registrations at the same time). Up in Scotland, Lanarkshire Tramways also had Brush bodies fitted to their Nos. 3–6, but these sat only 26 passengers. At the end of the war Bournemouth & District purchased a Daimler Y for bus work (No. 6, FX 4663).

Daimler KPL

DU 1251 must have been one of the strangest motorbuses ever to appear on our roads. Its designation is made up of the surname initials of the three engineers, who together planned this revolutionary vehicle, Messrs. *K*night, *P*ieper and *L*anchester.

It was in the summer of 1910 that the technical press was first introduced to this integral-constructed double-decker. 'The whole suspended parts of the vehicle are one homogeneous still structure,' ran a description at the time. DU 1251 had an overall length of 18 ft 10½ in., a track measurement of 6 ft 1 in. and a total height of 11 ft 9 in. Its wheelbase was 10 ft 5⅞ in. Perhaps it is not the roof canopy that to our eyes makes the whole machine appear so bizarre, but its wire wheels, the rear pair having a diameter of 48 in. compared with only 40 in. for the front ones.

The unladen weight of the KPL was 3 tons 9 cwt, but this included 5 cwt of accumulators, because another feature of this bus was its transmission system. It possessed an underfloor four-cylinder 12 h.p. Daimler-Knight engine, which was coupled with electromotors fitted to both rear driving wheels by means of worm and worm wheel. Yet another unusual item was the gearless nature of the KPL.

In May 1911 the Premier Motorbus Company was launched in London with the avowed object of operating a fleet of these advanced p.s.v's, but nothing came of this venture by reason of a successful patent action on behalf of the S.B. & S. syndicate. The KPL ran experimentally along the Hagley Road in Birmingham on behalf of the Birmingham and Midland Motor Omnibus Company (in other words 'Midland Red'). This occurred during November 1911 at a time when a great debate was going on locally as to whether this thoroughfare should have tram lines laid along it. Next month the Birmingham licensing authority gave Daimlers and Midland Red three months to prove their point. Meanwhile Weymouth Town Council anxious for some form of public transport showed an interest in the KPL, but eventually in the following year the G.W.R. were able to satisfy their needs. The KPL was obviously much in advance of its time.

De Dion-Bouton 2½-tonner

Any bus spotter in 1913 would have been able to identify a De Dion-Bouton 2½-tonner from a distance by its circular Solex radiator with its Mercedes-Benz style motif. With an overall length of 18 ft 8 in., the chassis had a wheelbase of 11 ft 8 in. and a ground clearance of 2 ft 7 in. It was powered by a four-cylinder engine with a bore of 100 mm and a stroke of 140 mm, and this was placed in such a position that the model was described as 'semi-forward drive'. A De Dion three-plate parallel disc metal-to-metal non-lubricated clutch was fitted, as in earlier De Dion models. There was a sliding pinion gearbox. The camshaft was chain driven, but the final drive was by means of De Dion worm. A prototype single-decker (LC 4195) was tried out by Road Motors Ltd. on their Luton to Letchworth route.

This 2½-tonner found favour down in the Poole area, where A. Knight & Co. used one as a charabanc in 1913 (FX 1870). Nearby, E. Poulain of Parkstone, having gained satisfaction whilst using his 1911 vintage 35 h.p. De Dion with so-called 'Torpedo' charabanc bodywork (FX 776) on his service to the Studland Ferry across the entrance of Poole

Harbour at Sandbanks, ordered others in 1912 (FX 1080), 1913 (FX 1546) and 1914 (FX 2139). Elliott of Bournemouth (of Royal Blue fame) purchased one in 1915 (EL 1718), while on the Isle of Man the Manx Electric Railway purchased one (MN 475) for excursion work in 1914.

F.I.A.T. 3-tonner

In March 1913 F.I.A.T. introduced into this country its new 3-tonner, rated at 30 h.p. This was powered by a four-cylinder engine with bore/stroke of 95 mm/180 mm (a huge stroke!). The multiple-disc clutch was retained. This model had a wheelbase of 11 ft 9 in. It was aimed at such operators as the North Eastern Railway Company, which already owned 18 F.I.A.Ts out of a total fleet of 48 in June 1912. Most of these were like BT 354 and BT 371, bearing charabanc bodies for excursion work at such seaside resorts as Bridlington and Scarborough, or that fashionable inland mecca, Harrogate.

Karrier A & B Series. Pl. 99, 100

Formed in 1907 as Clayton & Company, this manufacturer early adopted the trade name 'Karrier' for the products of its Huddersfield factory. Until 1911 Karriers were powered by two-cylinder engines of 18 h.p. As from 1909, passenger as well as goods vehicles were coming off the production lines. Final drive was by Coventry silent chains. There were basically four models:

Model	Control Position	Carrying Capacity
A/70	Forward	70 cwt
A/80	Forward	80 cwt
B/60	Normal	60 cwt
B/80	Normal	80 cwt

In 1911 a four-cylinder engine with bore/stroke of $4\frac{1}{8}$ in./$4\frac{1}{2}$ in. and rated at 22 h.p. was placed on the market. A. J. Middleton of Newcastle-under-Lyme took delivery of one of these as a P.A.Y.E. bus (E 1172). The B/6o was then being offered with a four-cylinder unit with bore/stroke of $4\frac{1}{2}$ in./$5\frac{1}{4}$ in., rated at 30 h.p. A demonstrator, CX 929, fitted with a 30-seat charabanc body, made an appearance at the North of England Show at Manchester in 1911. An alternative 40 h.p. engine was available, especially with the B/8o model, such as Tocia purchased in 1912 for its Pwllheli to Aberdaron route. These two vehicles with their single-deck rear-entrance bodies (CC 524 and CC 540), shared this service with a Karrier A/8o run by Nes & Griffiths (CC 547).

Staddons of Minehead had a special 50 h.p. Karrier charabanc built for them, and Y 2478 became the first p.s.v. to conquer the notorious 1 in 4 Porlock Hill in Somerset.

Lacre 1910 Range. Pl. 101

In January 1910 the Lacre Motor Car Company launched a whole range of models on to the British market. (The name Lacre was a contraction of Long Acre, the name of the street in which their head office was situated.) They varied in size from a 12-seater charabanc up to a 3-tonner suitable as a double-decker. The smallest of the Lacres had a two-cylinder engine of 12/15 h.p., and overall chassis length of 13 ft 5 in., a wheelbase of 9 ft and a width of 5 ft 11 in., the chassis weighing 20 cwt. Next in size came another two-cylinder version with an 18 h.p. engine. The overall chassis length was 17 ft 6 in., with a wheelbase of 12 ft and width of 6 ft 2 in. This 29 cwt chassis was claimed to be ideal for 20-seater charabanc work.

Perhaps the most popular of the Lacres of this period was the four-cylinder 30 h.p. model, with chassis dimensions of 20 ft (overall length), 13 ft 6 in. (wheelbase) and 6 ft 2 in. (width). This 32 cwt chassis was suggested as a 30-seater charabanc.

In Cornwall AF 798, bearing two less seats than the recommended total, plied between Falmouth and Penryn, whilst in Ireland UI 143 carried both passengers and mail from Londonderry to Greencastle. In North Wales the Cemaes Motor and General Agency ran EY 313 on the Isle of Anglesey, and named her 'Alma', while Brooke Bros. of Rhyl used DM 472 for excursion duties. In 1911 LA 739 of this type was ferried over to Ventnor in the Isle of Wight.

The double-deck chassis (or 3-tonner) had a 38 h.p. four-cylinder engine, an overall length of 19 ft and a wheelbase of 12 ft 6 in. Its width was the greatest of the series at 7 ft, whilst its weight was 44 cwt.

Leyland 'S' Series. Pl. 104–106

To cater for a demand for lighter vehicles the 'S' model was developed by Leyland. This had a 24 h.p. engine and weighed only 2 tons. Following the decision of the War Office to hold Subsidised Vehicle Trials in 1912 for a 3-ton chassis, a weightier model, the 'S3', was produced so as to earn a premium of £50 for each vehicle purchased, plus an annual subsidy of £20 for the first three years it was in service. The 'S3' had a four-cylinder 32 h.p. engine with a bore/stroke of $4\frac{1}{2}$ in./5 in., developing 46 b.h.p. at 1,800 r.p.m. The cylinders were cast in pairs and the timing gear was comprised of skew gears that were aimed at being quite silent. The braking system included a water-cooled footbrake operating on the cardan shaft. Variations followed in the 'S' series so that we find White Rose of Rhyl buying four classified as 'S4s' (DM 719/20, 1317 and 2127), whilst in 1912 Yorkshire Traction's Nos. 1–3 (HE 8–10), along with Edinburgh Corporation's Nos. 1–3 (S 4440–2) of 1914, were designated as 'S8s'. The latter had 29-seat rear-entrance bus bodies. By 1914 cast steel rear axles with double-reduction bevel-and-spur gear had been included in the modifications to the 'S' series. Production continued during the First World War, Eastbourne Corporation taking delivery of three with double-decker bodies in 1916 (Nos. 33–5, HC 1153/5/7).

A 36 h.p. version of the 'S' was known as the 'M'. This had an increased bore of 4⅝ in. Bournemouth & District Motor Services built up quite a fleet of 'Ms', fitted with bodywork by Kiddle, a firm that operated locally at Tuckton Bridge. The vehicles concerned were registered as EL 3984, 4006, 4432/3, 4496–8 and 4543/4.

On the double-decker front the 'X' was succeeded by the 'B' (in the same way as with A.E.C.!). This appears to have been powered by a 40 h.p. engine. The N.E.R. actually used 'Bs' for chara-banc work (e.g. BT 386), but Eastbourne Corporation had 38-seat double-deck bodies fitted to Nos. 31 (HC 223) and 32 (HC 245). Their Leyland bodywork had two-by-two seating in the lower saloon (as with the L.G.O.C./A.E.C. 'B'), instead of the more usual longitudinal benches. That was in 1912, and in 1914 five similar buses were bought (Nos. 33–7, HC 693/5/7/9/701). Meanwhile four went to Wellingborough Omnibus Company, who in 1917 sold LF 9875/8/9 and LF 9968 to Eastbourne Corporation.

Maudslay 3-tonner

From the Parkside, Coventry, factory of the Maudslay Motor Co. Ltd. issued forth in 1912 a new p.s.v. chassis, the 3-tonner, which was powered by a four-cylinder engine with bore/stroke of 4½ in./5 in., rated at 25/30 h.p. There was an overhead camshaft, and a vertical drive through two pairs of spiral gears. The final drive was by worm reduction of 7¾ to 1. The wheelbase of this model was 12 ft 6 in., and the chassis was fitted with 34 in. diameter wheels. Native Coventry Corporation bought six of these to start off its motorbus service. Nos. 1–6 (DU 258–63) had double-deck bodies. Ortona

of Cambridge also invested in one of these 3-ton double-deckers (DU 1752).

McCurd 3½-tonner. Pl. 107

Introduced late in 1912, this sturdy, straight chassis had a wheelbase of 13 ft 6 in., giving an overall chassis length of 20 ft. It was suitable, as so many heavier chassis were in those days, for both goods and passenger work. It was powered by a four-cylinder engine with a 4½ in. bore and a 5½ in. stroke, and this was rated at 42 b.h.p. at 1,080 r.p.m. The final drive was by worm to the rear axle.

Compared with other worm-driven chassis types, such as the longer established Dennis series, the McCurd did not find favour with the larger bus operators (we find it, for instance, in the newly formed fleet of Wilts. & Dorset Motor Service as their No. 6, IB 806), although two found their way into the ranks of the Brighton, Hove & Preston United Omnibus Company: CD 3322 received a single-deck bus body constructed by the operator, while its sister, CD 3327, was given a 30-seat charabanc body, built by Dodson.

Napier 2-tonner. Pl. 109

In 1913 Napier launched a 2-tonner with equal diameter wheels (at 900 mm). It had a wheelbase of 11 ft 6 in., and was powered by a four-cylinder engine with a 4 in. bore and a 6 in. stroke. A De Dion type single-plate clutch was fitted. Provincial purchased one of these from a Barnsley publican in 1913, and made it 24-seat charabanc No. 4 (MX 9751) in their Grimsby-based fleet.

In that year Napier placed on the market a 16/20 h.p. model with a reduced wheelbase of 9 ft 9 in., capable of seating sixteen passengers. It sold at £385, with an extra £100 for a body. R. M. Wright of Lincoln was one of the first operators of this smaller version with his FE 1068.

Ryknield 'R'. Pl. 110

In the summer of 1910 from the Burton-on-Trent stables came Ryknield's new 'R' type of 3-tonner. This was powered by a four-cylinder 40 h.p. engine that had a bore of 4¾ in. and a stroke of 5¼ in. The final drive was through encased external-toothed gearing and differential counter-shaft, which was carried on a triangular cross-sectioned perch bar. The tractive effort was transmitted through a spiral plate-spring fitted to the apex of the perch bar. The model displayed at the Manchester Show was fitted with a 30-seat charabanc body.

S.M.T. ordered four of the R, while the Mid-Derbyshire Motor Bus Company decided to purchase just one. Manchester Corporation bought two Rs (Nos. 3, N 4587 and 4, N 3635).

Scout 4-tonner. Pl. 111–114

In 1912 the Bemerton, Salisbury, factory of Scout Motors began to turn out bus chassis, and in August of that year they announced a 4-ton model powered by a four-cylinder engine with bore/stroke of 112 mm/140 mm and rated at 38 h.p. The final drive was by chains. There was a good clearance under the rear axle since this feature was essential for work on the uneven surfaces of country lanes at that time. One of the first Scout p.s.v's to take to the road was AM 2546 of 1912, which had a 30-seat front-entrance bus body with a central gangway and the seats in pairs, instead of the more usual arrangement of bench seats along the sides. J. Hall & Sons of Orcheston on Salisbury Plain, who traded as the Shrewton Motor Service, bought one Scout with a 27-seat charabanc body (complete with canvas roof), and another with a front-entrance bus body (AM 5363) in 1915. However, one of the best clients was the local Wilts. & Dorset Motor Services, which had bodies built by Marks of nearby Wilton for its Nos. 2–5 (IB 802–5), the first receiving a charabanc body (33 seats)

and the remainder 31- or 33-seat front-entrance single-deck bus bodies. No. 5 later passed into the ranks of Southdown Motor Services as its No. 92.

Two buses are quoted as 40 h.p. Scouts, but this may well be a misunderstanding. Brewer of Ringwood bought one with a Scout 30-seat front-entrance single-deck body in 1913 (IB 800?), whilst Provincial bought one with a double-deck body in 1915. No. 12 (?), EE 1160, passed into the ranks of Bartons after serving on Humberside. The new owners converted it to gas operation, placing the necessary storage bag on the top deck, thus making it for operational purposes into a single-decker.

Scout Motors did make a few smaller chassis described as 2/3-tonners and powered by a four-cylinder engine with a bore/stroke of 102 mm/140 mm. This is variously reported as 20 h.p. and 32 h.p. Shrewton Motor Service began its operations with such a vehicle, seating 20, in 1912. In 1914 Wilts. & Dorset's No. 1 (IB 801) received a 31-seat Marks single-deck bus body.

S.M.T. Lothian. Pl. 115, 116

In 1913, having for a number of years run Ryknields and Maudslays, the Scottish Motor Traction Company decided to design and build its own buses, and gave them the title 'Lothian'. The prototype S 3057 had an overall length of 23 ft but managed to accommodate 32 seated passengers; it included a seat facing backwards against the bulkhead and had a body divided into a forward non-smoking saloon and a rear smoking compartment. Another feature of the Lothian was the forward positioning of the driver in relation to the engine, whereby more passenger space was gained. The entrance at the rear of the vehicle had a cut-away appearance. The Lothian was powered by a 38h.p. Minerva Silent Knight four-cylinder engine with a four-speed gearbox, silent chain driven. The final drive was by worm. S 3057 entered service on the Uphall route in April 1913 bearing the Edinburgh licensing number 95. Whereas this prototype had a G. Hall & Co. (of Edinburgh) body, the rest of the Lothians had S.M.T. bodies, commencing with S 3597 (No. 55).

In 1915 a 31-seat charabanc version of the Lothian was produced for tours that started from Waverley Bridge, Edinburgh. By 1919, 44 Lothians had been built, and many of them had been fitted with a roof box containing a gas bag during the petrol shortage towards the end of the First World War. They were refilled at Penicuik Depot. At the time it was estimated that as well as the gas costing 2·17d. per mile to use, wear and tear accounted for a further 1·25d. per mile. The Lothians during our period were registered as they were built instead of in a block of Edinburgh numbers reserved for them, as the list below demonstrates:

S3597	S4400	S4836	S5697	S7618
S3662	S4543	S4846	S5862	S7715
S3703	S4617	S4849	S5916	S8461
S3841	S4654	S4851	S6423	S8533
S4068	S4655	S4963	S6729	S8594
S4100	S4716	S5224	S6761	S8668
S4287	S4748	S5496	S7063	S9102
S4288	S4770	S5550	S7322	S9103
S4399	S4813	S5595		

Eventually a further 45 Lothians were built, the last one (SF 504) making its debut in 1924.

Straker-Squire 'CO'

In 1913 Straker-Squire produced the further improved 'CO' version, and this found favour with Gateshead Tramways Company, who purchased several. J 2115 had an Immisch 34-seat double-deck body, while the remainder (J 2117–20/2) had forward-entrance single-deck bus bodies built by the same firm. The overall length of the 'CO' chassis was 19 ft 6½ in., with a wheelbase of 13 ft 6 in. The overall width was 7 ft 1¾ in., the whole chassis being made of pressed steel. The four-cylinder engine fitted to the 'CO' had a 4¼ in./5 in. bore/stroke rated at 28·8 b.h.p. A silent chain gearbox had only three forward and one reverse speed, compared with the multitude offered in the earlier models. Again, chains had been replaced by a cardan shaft and worm gearing. In Bedfordshire, Road Motors operated another 'CO' (D 5317) on its Luton to Leagrave route, whilst the B.H. & P.U.O.C. down in Sussex bought a further charabanc of this type (CD 3083), and later followed this up with modified COZ models (CD 3089) and several COTs (CD 3531/2/3 and IB 854–7) with a variety of bus and charabanc bodies built by Beadle, Dodson, Harrington and the operator itself. In addition in 1913 B.H. & P.U.O.C. had tried out an L.G.O.C. double-decked Straker-Squire (LN 4507). Douglas Corporation's No. 2 (MN 590) was also of this make, having a Strachans 22-seat rear-entrance bus body.

Thornycroft 'J'. Pl. 117

In the summer of 1913 Thornycrofts announced their new 3-tonner 'J' type commercial chassis. 'Springfield' writing in *Vintage Commercial* (October 1962) states that 'The Thornycroft engineers designed the "J" type to be simple, rugged, and generally reliable in arduous conditions.' The J was powered by a four-cylinder engine with a bore of 4½ in. and a stroke of 5 in. giving 30 h.p., although later the stroke was increased to 6 in., so that the unit could develop 40 h.p. The chassis had a wheelbase of 13 ft 7½ in. and a width of 7 ft 2½ in. The clutch was of the cone type lined by Ferodo. There was a four-speed gearbox with a gate change. Final transmission was through overhead worm gear to a live back axle. This feature had been laid down in the War Department specification for any vehicle wishing to qualify for a subsidy. A certificate to this effect had been issued by the War Office in January 1913. Altogether, over 5,000 Js were supplied to the Forces.

Bus operators were not really interested in the J until 1919, when Portsmouth Corporation and others bought Thornycrofts to restart or inaugurate motor bus routes. Across the harbour from Pompey, Provincial's subsidiary, the Gosport & Fareham Tramways Company, had started a motorbus route between Bury Cross and Lee-on-Solent in 1910 with a Thornycroft charabanc (AA 2473), and in 1914 they invested in a pair of Js. AA 5301 had a 28-seat charabanc body whilst AA 5302 apparently sat two more passengers, the latter vehicle ending her days with another member of the Provincial empire, the Cardiff Tramways Company. In 1919 Gosport & Fareham placed a repeat order for Js, and received HO 2301/2, following this up by three more (HO 2799 and HO 2910/11) the next year. The last mentioned actually had a chassis dating from 1915 (ex-War Dept. ?).

Tilling-Stevens TTA1. Pl. 118–120

In 1911, on 11 June, the prototype Tilling-Stevens TTA1 petrol-electric bus (LN 9998) entered service on Tillings Oxford Circus to Sidcup route. It was the first of a batch of TTA1s designed to replace 200 of the horse buses still being operated by Thomas Tilling. The four-cylinder engine had a bore/stroke of 105 mm/125 mm. *The Commercial Motor* described the method of transmission: 'The system consists of a petrol engine which is spring-coupled to a generator, whilst on the front end of the cardan shaft is a series-wound electric motor; the drive from this shaft is by worm-gearing to a live back axle; between the generator and the motor there is a powerful fan.' The generator had an

output of between 1 and 25 kilowatts at speeds varying from 350 r.p.m. up to 1,400 r.p.m. Unlike the earlier Hallford-Stevens S.B. & S. petrol-electric vehicle, this had only one motor instead of one for each rear wheel.

Birmingham Corporation bought thirteen TTA1s to replace some of the privately-owned horse buses still operating in the city. Nos. 0–12 (O 8200–12) had 34-seat double-deck bodies constructed by Brush. Newcastle upon Tyne Corporation also started off its motorbus fleet with TTA1s. It built its own double-deck bodies for BB 585–8. Liverpool Corporation was a third large municipality to do this with its double-deckers K 1591/2 and K 1631/2. Oldham Corporation bought a TTA1 (BU 11) as well. Over the border, the Greenock & Port Glasgow Tramways Company purchased a pair with Brush 34-seat double-deck bodies (VS 225/6), and these passed into the hands of S.M.T. in 1914.

A 40 h.p. version of the Tilling-Stevens petrol-electric appeared in 1913, designated the TTA2. Birmingham Corporation took another consignment with Nos. 13–29 (O 9913–29) with similar bodies to the 1912 batch. Neighbours Midland Red took a mixed bag of TTA2s. Nos. 1–7 (O 9930–6) and 20 (OA 2549) had 34-seat Brush double-deck bodies, whilst Nos. 8–13 (O 9937–42) had 27-seat rear-entrance Birch bodies, and Nos. 14–19 (OA 343–8) received 27-seat front-entrance Hora bus bodies. Oldham Corporation took into its fleet a further trio of 34-seat double-deckers (BU 69 and 401/2). BU 11 and BU 402 were sold to Warrington Corporation in 1917, when they were re-registered as ED 1180/1. There they joined three TTA2s delivered in 1913 with similar bodies (ED 615–17). In 1914 North Warwickshire bought a series of TTA2s, including AC 31 and E 1772, whilst the Greenock & Port Glasgow Tramways purchased another double-decker (V 2216). Incidentally VS 225/6 and V 2216 ended up in the Midland Red fleet as OA 7100–2 respectively. Walsall Corporation bought a pair of double-decked TTA2s in 1915 (DH 900/1), but Southend-on-Sea Corporation decided to have 22-seat single-deck bodies fitted to their three (HJ 28–30). The TTA2 (with a double-deck body) had an unladen weight of 4 tons 13 cwt.

In 1914 yet a third version of this petrol-electric appeared on the scene, the TS3. This came with a choice of two wheelbase lengths, viz. 13 ft 6 in. or 14 ft 6 in. This variation in wheelbase length helps to explain the considerable difference in body capacity between one TS3 and another of the same designation. Thus at one extreme, Thomas Tilling ran some 25-seat charabancs such as Nos. 552–4 (LH 7126, LH 8885 and LP 9667), and at the other Wolverhampton Nos. 9–12 (DA 3622–5) had English Electric 32-seat rear-entrance single-deck bus bodies, and Southdown 48 (CD 5648) and 50 (CD 2150) received 41-seat double-deck bodies built by L.G.O.C and Dodson respectively. As well as winning further patronage from Birmingham Corporation and Midland Red, the company sold four to Bournemouth Corporation in 1914: EL 2103/4 were given 34-seat Brush double-decker bodies, and EL 2105/6 had second-hand 24-seat rear-entrance Brush bodies that had formerly been carried by EL 366 and EL 480. Crosville No. 1 (M 5731) was a TS3 bearing a Tillings 36-seat double-deck body, whilst No. 2 (LH 9432) had a Dodson body of similar capacity. Across the Irish Sea, Douglas Corporation's No. 1 (MN 589) was a 25-seat single-deck bus on a TS3 chassis. Edinburgh Corporation Nos. 4–6 (S 4443–5) had 29-seat rear-entrance single-deck bus bodies. Wolverhampton Corporation had some rare Fleming 30-seat rear-entrance single-deck bodies fitted to their TS3s Nos. 7 (DA 2781) and 8 (DA 1551).

A.E.C. 50 Years, (A.E.C., 1962).

Barton Story, The, C. David Edgar, (Barton Transport, 1958).

Barton – Robin Hood, 3rd Edition, (East Midlands Area Omnibus Enthusiasts Soc., 1971).

Bath Tramways, Colin Maggs, (Oakwood Press, 1971).

Birmingham City Transport, Part 2: Buses, W. A. Camwell, (Ian Allan, 1950).

Birmingham, Early Omnibus Services in, 1834–1905, Alec G. Jenson, (Omnibus Soc.).

Birmingham & Midland Motor Omnibus Co. Ltd., Part I: 1904–1933, (Omnibus Soc. & P.S.V. Circle, 1961).

Birch Bros. Ltd and Luton Corporation Transport, (Omnibus Soc./P.S.V. Circle, 1970).

Bournemouth Corporation Transport, J. Mawson, (Advertiser Press, 1967).

Bradford Trolleybuses 1911–1960, A History of, Harold Brearley, (Oakwood Press, 1960).

Brighton & Hove, The Trolleybuses of, David Kaye & Martin Nimmo, (Reading Transport Soc., 1968).

British Bus Services, The History of, John Hibbs, (David & Charles, 1968).

Cheltenham's Trams & Buses 1890–1963, J. B. Appleby & F. Lloyd, (21 Tram Group, 1964).

Coaching Days and Coaching Ways, W. Outram Tristram, (Macmillan, 1903).

Coaching Times and After, Henfrey Smail, (Aldridge Bros., Worthing, 1948).

Early Motor Bus, The, Charles E. Lee, (British Railways Board, 1964).

Eastbourne Corporation Transport Department, 1903–1963, (Eastbourne Corp., 1963).

East Kent Buses and Coaches, S. L. Poole, (Ian Allan, 1949).

Eastern Municipalities, Motor Buses, Trolleybuses and Trams of the, (Omnibus Soc./P.S.V. Circle, 1969).

Fifty Years A Busman, D. Randall, (Town & Country Press, 1970).

First Thirty Years, The Story of the London Bus, 1904–1933, (Dryhurst, 1962).

Gosport & Fareham Omnibus Co. Ltd., (P.S.V. Circle/Omnibus Soc. 1971).

Hants. & Dorset Motor Services Ltd., Part I: 1916–1938, (Omnibus Soc./P.S.V. Circle, 1968).

Horse Bus as a Vehicle, The, Charles E. Lee, (British Railways Board, 1968).

Horse Drawn Carriages, (Glasgow Museum of Transport, 1968).

Hull Transport Museum Guide, (Hull Museums, 1968).

Inland Transport, 100 Years of, 1833–1933, C. E. R. Sherringham, (Cass, 1934, reprinted 1969).

Ireland, Transport in, 1880–1910, Patrick Flanagan, (Transport Research Associates, 1969).

Jersey, Transport in, 1788–1961, Michael Ginns, (Transport World, 1961).

Journey by Stages, Stella Margetson, (Cassell, 1967).

Journeys in England, Jack Simmons, (David & Charles, 1969).

Keighley Corporation Transport, J. S. King, (Advertiser Press, 1964).

Kingsland Road, A. W. McCall, (Omnibus Soc., 1961).

Lanarkshire Tramways, Ian L. Cormack, (Scottish Tramway Museum Soc., 1970).

Leeds City Transport, Fleet History of, (Leeds & Dist. Transport News, 1969).

Leyland: Seventy Years of Progress, (Leyland 1966).

London Country Bus, The, J. S. Wagstaff, (Oakwood Press, 1968).

London General, The Story of the London Bus, 1856–1956, (London Transport, 1956).

London Independent Bus Album, (Oakwood Press, 1969).

London Motor Bus, The, 1898–1968, R. W. Kidner, (Oakwood Press, 4th Edition, 1968).

London Transport, A History of, Vol. I: The Nineteenth Century, T. C. Barker & M. Robbins, (George Allen & Unwin, 1963).

London Trolleybuses, (Dryhurst, 1962).

Maidstone & District Motor Services Ltd., Buses & Coaches, (Ian Allan, 1950).

Manchester's Buses 1906–1945, Ralph Jackson (Manchester Transport Museum Society, 1972).

Midland Red Buses & Coaches, (Ian Allan, 1949).

Military Transport of World War I, C. Ellis & D. Bishop, (Blandford, 1970).

Omnibus, The, John Hibbs, (David & Charles, 1971).

Oxford, The City of, (Omnibus Soc., 1966).

Oxford Motor Services Ltd., City of, (Omnibus Soc./P.S.V. Circle, 1967).

Packhorse, Waggon and Post, J. Crofts, (Routledge & Kegan Paul, 1967).

Passenger Transport in Britain, The Story of, J. Joyce, (Ian Allan, 1967).

Plymouth Transport Centenary, 1870–1970, (Plymouth Bus Club, 1971).

Popular Carriage, (British Transport Commission, 1962).

Potteries Motor Traction Co. Ltd., (Omnibus Soc./P.S.V. Circle, 1967).

Reading, The Trolleybuses of, (Reading Transport Soc., 1966).

Rhondda Transport Co. Ltd., (Omnibus Soc./P.S.V. Circle, 1967).

Roads and their Traffic, 1750–1850, John Copeland, (David & Charles, 1970).

Roads and Vehicles, Anthony Bird, (Longmans, 1969).

Rolling Road, The, L. A. G. Strong, (Hutchinson, 1956).

Royal Blue Express Services, A History of the, R. C. Anderson & G. Frankish, (David & Charles, 1970).

Scottish Municipalities, Motor Buses & Trolleybuses of the, (Omnibus Soc./P.S.V. Circle, 1962).

Scout Motors of Salisbury, 1902–1921, Jeremy P. Farrant, (Salisbury & S. Wilts. Groups for Industrial Archaeology, 1968).

Southdown Motor Services Ltd., Buses & Coaches, (Ian Allan, 1950).

Southdown Motor Services Ltd., (Omnibus Soc./P.S.V. Circle, 1957).

Southdown Story, 1915–1965, (Southdown Motor Services, 1965).

South Eastern Municipalities, Motor Buses, Trolleybuses and Trams of the, (Omnibus Soc./P.S.V. Circle, 1969).

Stage Coach Services, 1836, A Directory of, Alan Bates, (David & Charles, 1969).

Stage-Coach to John o' Groats, Leslie Gardiner, (Hollis & Carter, 1961).

Steam on Common Roads, William Fletcher, (David & Charles reprint, 1972).

Tay Valley, Tramways of the, Alan W. Brotchie, (Dundee Museum & Art Gallery, 1965).

Technology, A History of, Vol. V. c. 1850–c. 1900, (Oxford U.P., 1958).

Teesside Trolleybuses, 50 Years of, 1919–1969, (National Trolleybus Assoc., 1969).

Thames Valley Traction Co. Ltd., (Omnibus Soc./P.S.V. Circle, 1960).

Transport: Visual History of Modern Britain, Jack Simmons, (Vista Books, 1962).

Transport Museums, Jack Simmons, (George Allen & Unwin, 1970).

Transport Preserved, Bryan Morgan, (British Railways Board, 1968).

Trolleybus Trails, J. Joyce, (Ian Allan, 1963).
Veteran & Vintage Public Service Vehicles, David Kaye, (Ian Allan, 1962).
Webb, H., Recollects, (Omnibus Soc., 1964).
Western Municipalities, Motor Buses & Trams of the, (Omnibus Soc./P.S.V. Circle, 1963).
West Midland Municipalities, Motor Buses, Trams & Trolleybuses of the Smaller, (Omnibus Soc./P.S.V. Circle, 1965).
Wheels of Service, P.M.T. 1898–1958, (Potteries Motor Traction, 1958).
Wilts. & Dorset Motor Services Ltd., (Omnibus Soc./P.S.V. Circle, 1963).
Worthing Road and its Coaches, Henfrey Smail, (Aldridge Bros., 1943).

INDEX